The New Adult's

Evening Journal

Life Skills for the Newly Minted

Michele Garner Press

First Edition 2025
Second Edition 2026

Printed in the United States of America.

ISBN 979-8-9990642-0-2

Library of Congress Control Number: Not available
This is a consumable work and has not been cataloged by the Library of Congress.

This Journal Belongs To

____

This book is dedicated to the class of 2025, especially to Tebogo, Lindsay, Danielle and Allison.

How to Use This Journal

This journal is not here to fix you, change you, or turn you into a productivity machine. It's here to **walk alongside you** during a year of transition - that strange stretch of time after high school when everything feels new, confusing, and a little intimidating.

Adulthood doesn't arrive all at once.
It's not a finish line you cross. It's something you build, piece by piece, often while sleep-deprived and asking AI how to boil eggs.

Each month in this journal explores a different emotional or mental skill that most of us don't get taught in school, like how to be alone without losing it, how to ask for help without spiraling, or how to take responsibility without collapsing into shame. You'll find:

- A theme for the month
- Short reflections to anchor you
- Writing prompts to help you go deeper
- Space to make it personal (no wrong answers here)

There is no perfect way to use this journal.
Write daily or weekly. Scribble in the margins. Skip months and come back later. Tear out pages if that's what helps. The only real "rule" is this: **Be honest with yourself. Gently.**

If you're here because someone gave this to you or because you picked it up not knowing what you needed, welcome. You're in exactly the right place. You don't need to be fully formed. You don't need to have it all figured out. This isn't about getting it "right." This is about showing up to your own life with curiosity, courage, and a pen.

Let's begin.

Table of Contents

Figuring Out Who You Are Without the Old Labels

Day 1

Who Named You?
From the moment we're born, people start naming us. They named us not just with our actual name but with other labels: the smart one, the quiet one, the troublemaker, the athlete. These labels often come from family, teachers or friends trying to make sense of who we are. Some might feel true, and others can feel like costumes we never chose. Today is about noticing the names you've been given, so you see how much space they take up.

What labels or roles have people used to describe you? Write down every label or role you've been given, big or small. Where did each one come from?

Just for this evening, I will be curious about the labels I've carried instead of assuming they all belong to me.

Day 2

Which Ones Fit?

Labels aren't all bad. Some remind us of our strengths and values. They can feel like home. Others stick to us long after they've stopped being true. Part of growing up is deciding which ones you want to keep and which ones you're ready to let go of.

Which labels feel true and supportive? Which ones feel false or outdated? Which ones do you know are true, and you want to let go of? Which one surprised you the most?

Just for this evening, I will give myself permission to let go of the names that no longer fit.

What do Labels Cost You?

Labels can shape the choices we make. You might avoid trying something because it doesn't match the "role" you've been given. Alternatively, you might overcompensate to prove a label wrong. Either way, it can feel like you're living inside someone else's script. Today is about noticing the power those scripts have on you.

Pick one of your labels. How has it shaped a choice you've made for better or worse?

Just for this evening, I will notice how much freedom I gain when I'm not living to meet someone else's expectation.

Day 4

The Silent Labels

Sometimes the labels that hold us back the most are ones we've given ourselves: "bad at relationships", "not creative", "too shy." These quiet labels can slip under the radar, guiding our choices without us even noticing. When you challenge them, you might find out they were never true to begin with.

What's a silent label you're carrying? What are three reasons why it might not be true anymore?

Just for this evening, I will remember that my thoughts are not always facts.

Day 5

Who Are You Without Them?

Imagine setting down all your labels for just one day, even the good ones. Who would you be, if you weren't trying to live up to an identity or disprove one? It might feel scary at first, but it can also feel like freedom. Let tonight be a small experiment in you being you, unboxed.

What would you do differently, if you weren't carrying any labels?

Just for this evening, I will let myself be who I am in this moment, without explanation or apology.

Day 6

More Than Your Resume

It's easy to define yourself by what you accomplish or produce: grade, jobs, hobbies, how helpful you are to others. Yet, those things don't tell the full story of who you are. Who you are is much deeper than what you do or achieve.

What are five things about yourself that have nothing to do with school, work, or responsibilities?

Just for this evening, I will remember that I am valuable simply because I exist.

The Danger of Performances

Sometimes we perform for approval without realizing it. We say, "yes" when we mean "no." We chase achievements we don't care about. We act in ways that keep us liked instead of authentic. It's not easy to step out of that pattern, but noticing it is the first step.

Where in your life do you feel like you're performing to be accepted?

Just for this evening, I will practice showing up as my real self, even in small ways.

Day 8

Your Worth Isn't Earned
You don't need to earn your worth by doing enough or being enough. It's a tough lesson to accept, especially when the world often rewards achievement over authenticity. Your worth was never meant to be something you prove. It's something you already have.

When do you feel like you're not enough? What would it look like to believe you already are?

Just for this evening, I give myself permission to be authentic without guilt.

Qualities Over Outcomes

What matters most isn't always what you accomplish but how you show up along the way. Qualities like kindness, curiosity, persistence, and integrity tell a truer story about who you are than any award or title ever could.

Which qualities do you value in yourself the most? When have you shown them in the last two weeks?

Just for this evening, I will focus on the kind of person I'm becoming, not just what I'm achieving.

Day 10

Rewriting the Story

Separating who you are from what you do takes practice. It may feel strange at first, because we're so used to introducing ourselves by our roles or accomplishments. However, you get to write a story about your life that goes deeper than any label or title.

Write your "who I am" statement using only values, qualities, or passions. Leave out schools, jobs, roles and achievements.

Just for this evening, I will choose to believe my identity is bigger than any single chapter in my life.

What Actually Matters to You?

Start asking "what matters to me?" You may realize you've been chasing things that matter more to other people than to you. Core values are the deep-down principles that guide your choices and shape how you want to live. Knowing them makes decisions clearer and life less reactive.

Write down five things you believe are most important in life. Don't overthink it.

Just for this evening, I will pay attention to what lights me up, not just what others expect.

Day 12

Values vs. the "Shoulds"

Sometimes we confuse "shoulds" with values. You might feel pressure to value success, popularity, or money, because that's what others seem to want. If those don't feel meaningful to you, they're not true values. They're expectations.

Which items on your list from yesterday are "shoulds" that you've inherited. Which truly feel like your own?

Just for this evening, I will honor what I value, even if it's different from the people around me.

What Do My Choices Reveal?

You can learn a lot about your values by looking at how you spend your time and energy. Do your choices align with the things you say matter most? If not, it's not a failure. It's information that can help you adjust.

Where in your life do your actions already line up with your values? Where do they feel out of sync?

Just for this evening, I will take one small step that reflects what matters most to me.

Day 14

Choosing Your Compass

Values act like a compass, helping you navigate decisions both big and small. You don't need to have them all figured out. Even choosing one or two to guide you right now can be enough.

If you could only choose three core values to live by this year, what would they be?

Just for this evening, I will let my choices flow from my values, not my fears.

Living From Your Values
Naming your values is just the beginning. Living from them is how you start building a life that feels like your own. Even small choices made with intention can shift how you feel day-to-day.

What's one value you want to lean more into over, say, the next week? How will you practice it in a tangible way?

Just for this evening, I will remember that small, value-driven choices add up to a meaningful life.

Day 16

When Roles Feel Too Small

As you grow, some roles you've played will start to feel too tight, like clothes you've outgrown. Maybe you were always the "responsible one," the "funny one," or the "quiet one." Now that role no longer fits. It's normal to feel conflicted about stepping out of something that once felt safe, even if it's holding you back.

What roles or identities feel too small for you now?

Just for this evening, I will allow myself to acknowledge what no longer fits without guilt.

The Fear of Disappointing Others

One reason we hold on to old roles is because we don't want to disappoint others. You might worry people will be upset if you stop being the "helper" or the "achiever." Staying trapped in a role just to keep others comfortable can cost you your authenticity.

Where are you holding onto a role because you're afraid of how others will react if you change?

Just for this evening, I will remember that my growth may make others uncomfortable. That's okay.

Day 18

Grieving the Old Version of You

Letting go of an identity can feel like grieving, even if it wasn't good for you. It's okay to miss the comfort and predictability of who you used to be. That version of you helped you survive. Now, you're learning how to thrive.

What do you need to grieve or say goodbye to in order to move forward?

Just for this evening, I will honor the version of me that got me here, even as I outgrow it.

Creating Space for the New You

When you release old roles, you make room for new ways of being. This can feel uncertain, but it's also exciting. Instead of rushing to define yourself, practice noticing what feels energizing and authentic now.

What makes you feel most like yourself right now, even in small moments?

Just for this evening, I will trust that letting go creates space for something better.

Day 20

Choosing Freedom Over Familiarity

It can be tempting to go back to familiar roles because they're comfortable. Growth happens outside of those old boxes. Freedom often feels awkward at first because you're not used to it. Over time, though, it starts to feel like home.

Where are you tempted to shrink back into the familiar? What would freedom look like instead?

Just for this evening, I will choose freedom, even if it feels uncertain.

Day 21

Permission to Experiment

You don't have to have your whole life figured out to start trying new things. This stage of life is meant for experimenting with interests, friendships, habits, and even how you express yourself. Each experiment teaches you something, even if you decide it's not for you.

What's something new you're curious about trying, even if you're not sure you'll be good at it?

Just for this evening, I will give myself permission to try without needing to be perfect.

Day 22

Following Energy, Not Expectations

Pay attention to what gives you energy, instead of what you think you "should" be doing. When you follow what excites or engages you, you'll discover parts of yourself you didn't know were there. Life doesn't have to be lived only by other people's checklists.

What activities, people, or experiences leave you feeling more alive?

Just for this evening, I will follow what feels energizing, not just what feels expected.

Trying On New Identities

You're allowed to try on different identities as you grow. That doesn't make you fake. It makes you flexible. It's how you discover what fits and what doesn't.

If you could step into a totally different "version" of yourself for a day, who would you be and what would you do?

Just for this evening, I will let myself explore different sides of who I am without judgment.

Day 24

Learning Through Mistakes

Trying new things means you will mess up sometimes. That's not failure. It's information. Each mistake teaches you something about what works for you and what doesn't. The only real mistake is staying stuck because you're afraid to try.

What's a mistake you've made recently, and what did it teach you about yourself?

Just for this evening, I will see mistakes as stepping stones and not as evidence that I'm failing.

Letting Curiosity Lead You
Curiosity is a powerful guide. When you let yourself follow the small sparks of interest you notice in everyday life, you'll uncover new passions and opportunities. You don't need to know where they'll lead. You just need to know that they're worth exploring.

What are you curious about right now? How can you take one small step toward it?

Just for this evening, I will follow my curiosity without needing a clear outcome.

Day 26

Identity is Not a Final Destination
It's easy to think your identity is something you "figure out" once and for all. Who you are is always changing, as it is shaped by your experiences and choices. Instead of chasing a final version of yourself, try seeing identity as something that grows with you.

Where have you already changed in ways you wouldn't have expected a year ago?

Just for this evening, I will allow my identity to grow and shift without forcing it to be final.

Day 27

Listening to Your Inner Voice

Other people's opinions will always be there, but the most important voice to listen to is your own. Your intuition is that quiet inner sense of what feels right for you. Your intuition is something you can strengthen over time. The more you practice listening, the clearer it gets.

When was the last time you ignored your inner voice? What would have happened if you'd trusted it instead?

Just for this evening, I will listen closely to what my inner voice is telling me.

Day 28

Defining Yourself by Your Values

Your values can anchor you when life feels uncertain. When you know what matters most to you, you don't need to cling to a rigid identity. You can move through the world in ways that stay true to those values, no matter what changes.

Which of your core values feel most important to live by right now?

Just for this evening, I will let my values and not my fears define who I am becoming.

Celebrating Who You Are Now

It's easy to focus on who you want to be in the future and forget to appreciate who you are now. Growth matters, and so does pausing to see how far you've already come. Take a moment to acknowledge the version of you who's reading these words. You're already worth celebrating.

What are three things about yourself right now that you appreciate?

Just for this evening, I will celebrate who I am today and not just who I might be tomorrow.

Day 30

A Living, Breathing You

Who you are is not fixed. You're allowed to change your mind, evolve your interests, and rewrite your story as many times as you need. This section has been about seeing yourself clearly and giving yourself permission to grow.

How do you want to keep showing up for yourself as your identity continues to evolve?

Just for this evening, I will remember that becoming is a lifelong process. I'm allowed to enjoy it.

Who You're Becoming

This chapter has been about looking closely at who you've been told you are, letting go of roles that no longer fit, and exploring who you're becoming. You've done the work of questioning labels, naming your values, and allowing your identity to evolve. The truth is this: you don't need to have it all figured out. You just need to keep showing up for yourself. Who you are is not a fixed destination but a living, growing part of you.

Looking back over this section, what have you discovered about yourself? How do you want to carry these lessons forward into the rest of your journey?

Just for this evening, I will honor the work I've done this chapter and step into the next one with curiosity and confidence.

Dealing with Uncertainty

Day 32

Where Are You Now?

Uncertainty is one of the hardest parts of adulting. You might not know where life is headed, what the right decision is, or whether things will work out the way you hope. This chapter is about learning how to live with that uncertainty without letting it control you.

Where do you currently feel the most uncertain in your life? How does it show up for you? For example, does it show up as worry, indecision, procrastination, or something else?

Just for this evening, I will be honest with myself about where I feel unsure. I accept that awareness is the first step.

Day 33

Naming It

Uncertainty often shows up as a vague, heavy feeling in the background. When you name it, it loses some of its power. You can start to see it clearly, instead of letting it control your choices from the shadows.

What areas of your life feel uncertain right now? Be as specific as you can.

Just for this evening, I will remind myself that naming my fears doesn't make them bigger. It makes them easier to face.

How You Usually Respond

Everyone has a default way of handling uncertainty. Some people avoid it. Others overthink or try to control everything. When you notice your patterns, you can start to respond differently.

How do you usually react when you don't know what's going to happen? What's your "go-to" response?

Just for this evening, I will notice my patterns without judging myself for them.

Day 35

The Stories You Tell Yourself
Uncertainty is often less about the situation and more about the story you tell yourself about it. Do you assume the worst? Do you tell yourself you can't handle it? Changing the story can change how you feel.

What story do you tell yourself when life feels uncertain? Is it helping you or hurting you?

Just for this evening, I will question the stories I tell myself and choose ones that support me.

Accepting That Uncertainty is Normal

It's easy to believe you're failing, when you don't have all the answers. Uncertainty is part of everyone's life. Even the most "together" people don't know what's coming next.

Where have you believed that uncertainty means you're doing something wrong?

Just for this evening, I will remember that life's uncertainty is a shared human experience.

Day 37

What You Can and Can't Control

Not all uncertainty can be resolved, but you can focus on what you do have power over. This doesn't mean ignoring what you can't control. It means choosing where to put your energy.

What parts of your current uncertainty can you influence, and what is truly outside your control?

Just for this evening, I will focus my energy on what I can change and release what I can't.

Shifting Perspective

Uncertainty isn't just about fear. It can also be about possibility. The same unknown that makes you anxious also holds potential you can't see yet.

Where could uncertainty in your life be opening the door for something good or unexpected?

Just for this evening, I will practice seeing uncertainty as a space for growth and new possibilities.

Day 39

Uncertainty Is a Mirror

Uncertainty doesn't just show you the world. It shows you yourself. When life is unpredictable, you're forced to confront how you handle fear, control, vulnerability, and trust. Instead of thinking of uncertainty as something happening *to* you, try seeing it as something that reveals who you are and what you believe.

What has uncertainty shown you about yourself lately? Has it shown you that you avoid it, try to control it, feel energized by it, or something else entirely?

Just for this evening, I will let uncertainty teach me something about myself instead of trying to push it away.

Why Discomfort Matters

Our instinct is to avoid discomfort, but learning to tolerate it makes you stronger. You can't control the unknown, but you can build your ability to sit with it without panicking.

What's one time you stayed with discomfort instead of avoiding it? What happened?

Just for this evening, I will remind myself that discomfort isn't danger. It's growth.

Day 41

Grounding Yourself in the Present

Uncertainty pulls your mind into the future, but the present moment is where you have the most power. Simple grounding practices can help bring you back. Try noticing your breath or feeling your feet on the floor until you can feel yourself in the present moment.

What helps you feel grounded when your thoughts spiral about the future?

Just for this evening, I will come back to the present moment when my mind drifts too far ahead.

Practicing "I Don't Know Yet"
It's okay not to have all the answers. Saying "I don't know yet" takes the pressure off and creates space for clarity to develop over time.

Where in your life could you practice saying, "I don't know yet," instead of forcing certainty?

Just for this evening, I will give myself permission to not know everything right now.

Day 43

Releasing the Need for Perfect Timing

Uncertainty often makes you wait for the "perfect moment" to act, but that moment rarely comes. Small, imperfect steps forward can build confidence, even when you don't have it all figured out.

Where have you been waiting for certainty before moving forward? What's one step you could take now?

Just for this evening, I will choose action over waiting for a perfect plan.

Learning to Self-Soothe

When uncertainty feels overwhelming, it helps to have healthy tools that calm your body and mind. Taking deep breaths, journaling, calling a trusted friend, or even going for a walk can help you regulate instead of react.

What soothes you when you're anxious about the unknown? How can you make it a healthy habit?

Just for this evening, I will care for my nervous system as much as I care for my to-do list.

Day 45

Finding Safety Inside Yourself

The more you trust yourself, the less scary uncertainty becomes. When you know you can handle whatever comes, you don't need life to be predictable.

What strengths or qualities do you have that help you handle change?

Just for this evening, I will trust that I can meet the future with the tools I already have.

Discomfort Has Boundaries

Not all discomfort is dangerous. Some of it is just your nervous system stretching and adjusting to a new level of uncertainty. The more you get familiar with what's uncomfortable but safe, the more capacity you build to stay present through hard things.

What types of discomfort are actually tolerable, even if they're unpleasant? How can you tell the difference between "stretch" and "too much?"

Just for this evening, I will honor the difference between discomfort I can grow from and pain I need to step away from.

Day 47

Holding Plans Loosely

Having a plan can give you a sense of control. Clinging to it too tightly can backfire. Life will shift and surprise you, and flexibility is what lets you adapt instead of break.

Where in your life are you trying to force a plan that might not be working anymore?

Just for this evening, I will hold space for both structure and spontaneity.

Day 48

Letting Go of "Either/Or" Thinking

Uncertainty loves to trick you into thinking there are only two options: success or failure, right or wrong, yes or no. Most of life exists in the messy middle. When you stop needing everything to be black and white, you make room for creativity.

Where are you seeing a situation as either/or? What possibilities are in the "both/and"?

Just for this evening, I will stay open to the space between extremes.

Day 49

Curiosity Over Control

You don't need to control everything. You can be curious instead. Asking "What's happening here?" instead of "How do I fix this?" softens your experience and keeps you from spiraling.

What's one uncertain part of your life you could approach with curiosity instead of control?

Just for this evening, I will practice replacing panic with curiosity.

Breaking the Rules You Made Up

Sometimes we operate by rules that were never actually real. Here are a few examples: "I have to be productive to be valuable," "I can't change my mind," "I should have it all figured out by now." These stories limit your flexibility and add unnecessary stress.

What personal "rules" are you following that might no longer serve you?

Just for this evening, I will give myself permission to rewrite the rules.

Day 51

Learning to Pivot

When plans change or doors close, it means it's time to pivot. Pivoting is a skill. It means shifting your energy while staying connected to your deeper values.

When was the last time you had to pivot in your life? What did it teach you?

Just for this evening, I will honor my ability to adapt and grow, even when things don't go as planned.

Day 52

Listening for New Information

As things unfold, new information becomes available, if you're open to seeing it. Uncertainty doesn't mean you're stuck. It means you're still gathering pieces of the puzzle.

What's something new you've noticed or learned this chapter that shifted your thinking?

Just for this evening, I will stay open to the possibility that I don't know everything … yet.

Day 53

Openness Is a Practice

Being open isn't about being passive. It's an active choice to stay curious instead of shutting down. Flexibility doesn't mean you don't care. It means you're willing to be changed by what you discover. It means staying in motion, even when you don't know where it's leading yet.

Where in your life could you practice being open to something unfamiliar, even if it's just for a moment?

Just for this evening, I will make space for something unexpected to surprise me … in a good way.

You Don't Need to Be Certain to Act

Confidence doesn't mean knowing the outcome. It means trusting you can handle whatever happens. You don't have to wait until you feel 100% ready to move. You can move while still feeling unsure.

Where are you waiting for "clarity" before acting? What's a small step you could take anyway?

Just for this evening, I will trust that progress can begin before certainty arrives.

Day 55

Building Evidence That You're Capable

Take a look back into your past. You've already faced uncertainty and made it through. The more you notice your own resilience, the easier it becomes to move forward even when you're scared.

What's one moment from your past where you handled uncertainty better than you expected?

Just for this evening, I will let my past strength remind me that I'm capable.

Taking Imperfect Action
The best way to build momentum is to take action. Take action even if it's messy, small, or unclear. Waiting for perfect conditions only feeds anxiety. You learn more by doing than by overthinking.

What's one imperfect action you could take this week that would move you forward?

Just for this evening, I will choose motion over perfection.

Day 57

Creating Your Own Anchors

In uncertain times, having internal anchors like values, routines, and people you trust helps you stay grounded. They won't eliminate the unknown, but they'll keep you steady when things feel unmoored.

What anchors help you feel secure when life feels chaotic? How can you return to them more often?

Just for this evening, I will reconnect to what steadies me.

Rebuilding Trust in Yourself

Self-trust grows each time you show up for yourself. When you listen to your needs, honor your boundaries, and take thoughtful risks, you send the message: I can trust myself to handle this.

What's one way you've earned your own trust lately?

Just for this evening, I will trust myself more than my fears.

Day 59

Defining Success Differently

Success isn't always clarity, results, or ease. Sometimes success is trying, showing up, staying kind, or simply not giving up. You get to define what it looks like for you, especially when the future is blurry.

What does success look like for you when things are uncertain?

Just for this evening, I will let my definition of success reflect what matters most to me.

Courage Isn't Loud

Courage doesn't always look like a bold leap. Sometimes it's quietly showing up when you'd rather hide. Sometimes it's making a phone call, submitting an application, or asking a hard question. You don't need to feel ready. You just need to be willing.

What's one small, quiet act of courage you've taken lately? What did it cost you to take it?

Just for this evening, I will give myself credit for the quiet bravery it takes to keep going.

Day 61

What Did You Learn?

This chapter has asked a lot of you. It's asked you to slow down, to notice, and to stay present with what's unclear. You've explored your relationship with uncertainty, learned to stay grounded, and practiced moving forward without all the answers. That's brave, and it's worth honoring.

What have you learned about yourself through completing this section? How will you carry it forward into your next chapter?

Just for this evening, I will recognize how far I've come and walk into next chapter with trust in who I'm becoming.

Learning to Be Alone Without Feeling Lonely

Where Are You with Being Alone?

We all have a relationship with being alone. Some people crave it, others avoid it, and many of us bounce between the two depending on the day. This chapter is about shifting the experience of solitude from something empty and uncomfortable into something grounding and nourishing. You'll learn how to spend time with yourself, not because you have to, but because you want to.

At this time in your life, how do you feel when you're alone? What emotions or thoughts usually show up?

Just for this evening, I will be honest about my relationship with solitude, even if it feels complicated.

Day 63

They Are Not the Same Thing

Loneliness and solitude are not the same. Loneliness is the ache of disconnection from others or from yourself. Solitude is the act of choosing stillness, space, and self-presence. Today, start noticing the difference.

When have you felt lonely even while surrounded by people? When have you felt okay (or even good) being alone?

Just for this evening, I will begin to notice when I'm truly lonely and when I'm simply alone.

Loneliness Is a Signal, Not a Flaw

Loneliness isn't proof that something's wrong with you. It's a message that says, "You're craving connection." That connection might be with others, with purpose, or even with yourself. What matters is how you respond to it.

What does loneliness tend to signal for you? How do you usually react to it?

Just for this evening, I will treat my loneliness as information and not as a character flaw.

Day 65

The Fear of Emptiness
Sometimes, we fear being alone because it means we'll have to face what's under the noise: thoughts, memories, silence. What if the emptiness you're avoiding is actually the doorway to your truest self? Stillness can be uncomfortable, but it's not dangerous.

What are you afraid might surface when things get quiet? What might you find there that could surprise you?

Just for this evening, I will allow a little stillness, not because I have to, but because I'm strong enough to face it.

When Loneliness Comes and Goes

Loneliness isn't always constant. Sometimes it creeps in during transitions, slow weekends, or unstructured hours. The goal isn't to banish it entirely. It's to learn how to move through the feeling without letting it define you. It's okay if it comes. It's okay if it passes.

What are the times or situations where loneliness tends to visit you? What helps soften it?

Just for this evening, I will remember that loneliness is a visitor and not a permanent state.

Day 67

The Difference Between Attention and Connection

Social media, texts, and likes are forms of attention but not always connection. You can be surrounded by notifications and still feel deeply alone. What you're craving might not be more noise. What you're craving might be more realness.

What kinds of interaction leave you feeling full? Which ones leave you still hungry?

Just for this evening, I will seek connection and not just attention.

Aloneness Can Be Sacred

Being alone doesn't have to feel like a gap. It can feel like a sanctuary. When no one's watching, you can breathe differently, think differently, and be differently. There's a freedom in solitude that no crowd can give.

What would it feel like to treat your alone time as sacred, rather than as something to escape?

Just for this evening, I will treat my time with myself like it matters because it does.

Day 69

Loneliness Doesn't Define You

Feeling lonely doesn't mean you're broken or unlovable. It means you're human. You're allowed to want connection and learn to enjoy solitude. You don't have to pick one or the other.

What story have you been telling yourself about what it means to be lonely? What if that story isn't true anymore?

Just for this evening, I will hold space for both solitude and connection in my life.

Being With Yourself Without Distracting Yourself

We're taught to fill every empty moment. So, we fill it with scrolling, sound, multitasking, and more. Presence isn't about being busy. It's about being with yourself. The next few days are about learning to do that gently without needing to escape.

What's one moment today when you caught yourself reaching for distraction? What were you trying to avoid?

Just for this evening, I will try spending five quiet minutes being present with myself without distractions.

Day 71

You Are Not Boring

If you're afraid to spend time alone, it might be because you worry that you're boring. Or, perhaps worse, you're afraid that you'll be bored by your own mind. You are not boring. You just might not have had the chance to really get to know yourself without performance or noise.

What do you enjoy doing when no one else is around to judge, watch, or approve?

Just for this evening, I will notice what brings me joy when no one is looking.

Comfort Isn't Always Instant

Getting comfortable with yourself takes practice. The first time you eat out alone, go on a solo walk, or spend a whole evening with your thoughts might feel awkward. That's okay. Discomfort doesn't mean you're doing it wrong. It means you're doing something new.

When have you done something alone that felt uncomfortable at first but grew easier over time?

Just for this evening, I will allow space for awkwardness to become ease.

Day 73

Talking to Yourself Like You Matter

You spend more time with yourself than with anyone else. So, how you talk to yourself matters. Your inner voice can either be a bully or a best friend. You get to choose which one shows up.

How do you speak to yourself when no one else can hear? Would you say those things to someone you love?

Just for this evening, I will speak to myself with the care I'd give a dear friend.

Creating a Ritual Just for You

One way to become more comfortable in your own company is to build rituals that are yours and yours alone. Try something small, meaningful, and quiet that is a way to say, "I matter to me."

What's a simple ritual you could create to enjoy your alone time? Perhaps it's something you look forward to, even if it's just five minutes long.

Just for this evening, I will create a moment for myself that no one else needs to understand.

Day 75

Your Own Space as an Act of Self-Love

Whether it's a corner of a room, a notebook, or a playlist, your personal space can become a soft place to land. It doesn't have to be big. It just has to be yours. Making space for yourself is a signal that you belong to you.

Where do you feel most safe or "yourself?" How can you make that space more nurturing?

Just for this evening, I will make space for myself.

Day 76

You're Allowed to Enjoy Your Own Company

It's not selfish, weird, or antisocial to love your alone time. In fact, when you enjoy your own company, your relationships become stronger because they're built on choice, not dependency.

What's one thing you truly enjoy doing alone that you want to make more time for?

Just for this evening, I will allow myself to love being with me.

Day 77

Who's Talking Here?

You have an inner narrator. It's that constant voice in your head that comments, worries, plans, judges, and remembers. The question isn't whether that voice exists, but whether it's kind, honest or helpful. Getting to know it is the beginning of self-connection.

If you paused right now, what's one thing your inner voice is saying? Is the nature if your inner voice supportive, critical, anxious, curious, or something else?

Just for this evening, I will pay attention to my inner voice without letting it run the show.

Turning the Volume Down

Sometimes the voice in your head gets loud … too loud. It spins, obsesses, replays conversations, and worries about things that haven't happened. You don't have to believe every thought you think. You can slow down and choose which ones deserve your attention.

What's a recurring thought that's been taking up too much space in your head lately? Is it true or just loud?

Just for this evening, I will remind myself that not every thought deserves a response.

Day 79

What Do You Actually Need?
Beneath the noise, you always have needs. You have needs for rest, for validation, for connection, and for stillness. When you learn to hear what you need, you can care for yourself with intention instead of reaction on autopilot.

What's something your body, mind, or heart has been asking for lately, even if you've been ignoring it?

Just for this evening, I will ask myself what I need and try to offer myself a small piece of it.

Your Inner Critic Isn't the Boss

Have you heard that harsh voice inside? It's the one that says you're not doing enough, not good enough, not lovable enough? It's loud, but it's not wise. Often, the "not enough" voice is just fear in disguise. You get to choose who you trust inside your own head.

What's one thing your inner critic tends to say? How would you respond to a friend who said about themselves?

Just for this evening, I will speak to myself the way I wish someone else would speak to me.

Day 81

Becoming a Better Inner Friend

When you're alone, your inner voice is your main companion. It helps to make it a good one. Self-connection grows when you stop criticizing yourself and start relating to yourself with warmth, humor, and care.

What would it look like to befriend yourself this week? What would it look like to not just take care of yourself, but *like* yourself this week?

Just for this evening, I will treat myself like someone worth spending time with.

Listening Without Fixing

Sometimes, the best kind of self-connection isn't about fixing or solving. Sometimes it's just about witnessing. Sit with your own feelings without judging them. Let yourself be sad, or tired, or uncertain without immediately needing to push through it.

What feeling have you been trying to fix, silence, or skip over? What might happen if you just let it be for a while?

Just for this evening, I will sit with what's true without rushing it away.

Day 83

Coming Home to Yourself

You are your own home. No matter where you go, who you're with, or what's happening around you, you are always there. The more you practice coming back to yourself with compassion, the less lonely aloneness becomes.

What helps you feel connected to yourself? How can you return to that more often?

Just for this evening, I will treat myself like home and not like a project to be fixed.

The Line Between Solitude and Isolation

Solitude is chosen. Isolation is when you feel trapped in your aloneness. The difference often comes down to intention. Are you withdrawing to restore or because you feel like no one sees you? Learning to recognize the difference helps you stay connected, even while spending time on your own.

When does your alone time feel nourishing, and when does it start to feel like disconnection? What signals that you've crossed that line?

Just for this evening, I will notice the difference between quiet and disconnect.

Day 85

You Still Belong

Being alone doesn't mean you're on the outside of everything. You still belong to your communities, your friendships, and your dreams. You don't stop being part of the world just because you're spending time in your own orbit.

Where in life do you feel a sense of belonging, even when you're not physically with others?

Just for this evening, I will remind myself that I am still connected, even in stillness.

The Myth of Constant Connection

Modern life makes it seem like you should always be available, always replying, or always online. Too much connection without space can leave you overwhelmed, fragmented, and even lonelier. Sometimes solitude is the reset that brings you back to authentic connection.

What's one way the constant connection has been draining you? Where might a little intentional solitude help you reconnect to yourself?

Just for this evening, I will step away from the noise and remember that connection starts with presence.

Day 87

Relationships That Make Room for Solitude

Healthy relationships respect your need for alone time. If someone takes it personally when you need space, that's not love. That's control or fear. The people who truly care about you will support your growth, even when it means stepping back to breathe.

Are there relationships in your life that allow you to take space without guilt? Are there any that don't? What does that tell you?

Just for this evening, I will trust that real connection doesn't disappear just because I take a moment for myself.

Designing Your Life to Include Quiet

If you wait for the world to hand you quiet moments, you might be waiting a long time. The pace of everything will try to fill every hour. Still, you can build a life that includes intentional, protected space a rhythm rather than an escape.

What would it look like to design your days with a little more intentional solitude, even for ten minutes at a time?

Just for this evening, I will choose a moment of stillness and treat it like it matters.

Day 89

People Who Feel Like Solitude

Some people drain you. Others leave you feeling like you've just come home. They leave you feeling calm, seen, and fully yourself. These are the kinds of relationships that complement solitude rather than compete with it.

Who in your life helps you feel grounded, rather than overstimulated or performative? What makes those relationships different?

Just for this evening, I will value relationships that leave me feeling more like myself.

Being Alone in a Connected Life

The goal isn't to live in total solitude or to avoid being alone. It's to create a life where both connection and alone time exist in balance. Solitude becomes powerful when it's a choice and not a sentence. You get to decide how it fits into your life.

What does a healthy balance of solitude and connection look like for you right now? What needs adjusting?

Just for this evening, I will remember that alone time is something I get to choose and shape for myself.

Day 91

Your Relationship with Yourself Deserves Ritual

You make time for birthdays, meetings, and social plans. Do you make time for yourself? You deserve rituals that are yours and that signal you matter, even when no one's watching. A ritual doesn't need to be elaborate. It just needs to be intentional.

What small daily or weekly ritual could help you feel grounded, seen, or cared for … even if it only takes five minutes?

Just for this evening, I will treat my time with myself as worthy of ritual and rhythm.

What You've Learned About Being with Yourself

You've spent the past 30-some days redefining what it means to be alone. You've examined the difference between loneliness and solitude, learned to build comfort in your own presence, practiced kindness in your inner dialogue, and started creating moments that honor your worth. Being alone doesn't mean being forgotten, broken, or unloved. It means learning how to be present with yourself without needing to escape. It's about becoming someone you trust, someone you enjoy, and someone you know.

What feels different now about your relationship with solitude than it did at the start of this chapter? Where have you surprised yourself? What are you still growing into?

Just for this evening, I will honor the quiet strength it takes to truly keep myself company.

Taking Responsibility Without Shame Spiraling

What Does Responsibility Mean to You?
For new adults, learning how to take responsibility without drowning in guilt, embarrassment, or fear is a game changer. This chapter is about owning your choices, repairing mistakes, and showing up for yourself in a way that builds trust instead of shame.

The word "responsibility" can carry a lot of weight. Maybe it reminds you of getting blamed for something. Maybe it makes you think of pressure, punishment, or trying not to disappoint people. Real responsibility isn't about being perfect. It's about showing up honestly. It's about learning from your actions without beating yourself up.

When you hear the word "responsibility," what comes up for you in terms of feelings, stories, and expectations? How would you define it today?

Just for this evening, I will be open to rewriting my definition of responsibility as one that leaves room for growth, not shame.

Day 94

Not the Same Blame

Responsibility and blame are not the same. Blame is reactive. It points fingers, looks backward, and often leads to shame. Responsibility is responsive. It looks forward and asks, *"What can I learn? What can I do now?"*

Where in your life have you confused blame with responsibility? How does that change the way you respond to mistakes?

Just for this evening, I will explore what it means to be responsible without punishing myself.

You're Not the Only One Learning

Taking responsibility can feel especially hard when you assume that everyone else has it figured out. Here's the truth: most people are learning as they go. Owning your part in something doesn't make you the worst. It makes you someone who's growing.

What would change if you stopped assuming that being wrong means being "bad?"

Just for this evening, I will allow myself to be learning and stop striving to be flawless.

Day 96

The Freedom of Owning It

Avoiding responsibility might feel easier at first. Eventually, it usually leads to stress, shame, or disconnection down the road. When you own your actions, you gain clarity, freedom, and self-respect. Responsibility is a way of getting unstuck.

What's something small you've been avoiding taking responsibility for and what might shift if you simply owned it?

Just for this evening, I will take one small step toward freedom by naming what's mine to carry.

Day 97

You're Allowed to Try Again
Taking responsibility doesn't mean your one chance is over. In fact, responsibility creates more chances to grow, to repair, and to show up differently next time. The goal isn't perfection. It's showing up again with intention.

Where are you holding yourself to a standard that doesn't leave room for trying again?

Just for this evening, I will remind myself that mistakes don't cancel my potential.

Day 98

Owning Your Choices Without Justifying Them

It's easy to explain away your actions. "I was tired." "They started it." "I didn't know what else to do." While context matters, taking responsibility means being honest about what you chose, even when there were hard circumstances.

What's a moment where you've caught yourself making excuses instead of owning a decision? What would it feel like to name it honestly?

Just for this evening, I will practice honest reflection without self-defense.

Responsibility Grows with Power

The more choices you're able to make for yourself, the more responsibility you carry. This isn't punishment. It's agency. Owning your influence means you get to shape your outcomes, your relationships, and your world.

Where in your life are you ready to take more responsibility … not because you "have to," but because it gives you more power to direct your life?

Just for this evening, I will remember that responsibility is a form of freedom.

Day 100

Responsibility Includes Being Kind to Yourself

It's easy to think responsibility means beating yourself up, but real responsibility includes self-compassion. You're more likely to grow when you feel safe with yourself and less likely when you feel ashamed. The goal isn't to tear yourself down. It's to build yourself up with honesty and care.

How can you practice responsibility and self-kindness at the same time, even when you've messed up?

Just for this evening, I will treat myself like someone who is capable and still learning.

Mistakes Are How You Learn

Making mistakes doesn't mean you've failed at life. It means you're in it. Nobody learns without getting some things wrong first. Instead of asking, "Why did I screw this up?" try asking, "What is this showing me?" That's how growth happens.

What's a recent mistake you made that's still lingering in your mind? What might it be trying to teach you?

Just for this evening, I will see mistakes as teachers and not enemies.

Day 102

Panic ≠ Accountability

Freaking out about a mistake can feel like taking it seriously, but panic doesn't equal accountability. Melting down doesn't make you more responsible. You can take ownership without tearing yourself apart.

When you mess up, do you tend to freeze, spiral, or go into fix-it-overdrive? What would a calmer version of accountability look like for you?

Just for this evening, I will let accountability feel steady.

Everyone Messes Up ... Even People You Admire

The people you look up to? They've all said the wrong thing, missed a deadline, let someone down, or made a choice they regret. What makes them admirable isn't perfection. It's what they did next.

Think of someone you admire. What's a mistake they've made that you know about, and how did they move forward from it?

Just for this evening, I will remind myself that I'm not alone in messing up.

Day 104

You Don't Have to Earn Forgiveness with Self-Punishment
It's easy to believe that, if you hurt someone or dropped the ball, you have to punish yourself to "make it right." Shame doesn't create healing. It creates stuckness. You can be responsible and kind to yourself at the same time.

Where have you been holding on to guilt longer than you need to? What would it take to loosen your grip?

Just for this evening, I will remember that beating myself up isn't the same as making things better.

Mistakes Don't Define You

One moment doesn't undo who you are. One decision, one awkward conversation, one forgotten task, or one bad day doesn't cancel out everything else about you. You are still a full person, even when you mess up.

What's one mistake you've let define you for too long? What else is true about you beyond that moment?

Just for this evening, I will hold space for the whole story and not just the hardest chapter.

Day 106

Apologies Aren't Shame Missions
Apologizing isn't about humiliating yourself or begging for acceptance. It's about acknowledging the impact of your actions and showing up with honesty and care. A real apology holds both regret and self-respect.

What makes apologizing hard for you? How can you offer one without losing your sense of self?

Just for this evening, I will see apologies as a bridges instead of as burdens.

Your Nervous System Matters, Too
When you mess up, your body often reacts first. Your chest tightens. Your mind spins. Your stomach flips. Before you rush to fix anything, take care of your nervous system. Regulating yourself is not a delay. It's responsible.

What helps you calm down when you're overwhelmed by a mistake? How can you practice that more intentionally next time?

Just for this evening, I will slow down enough to respond instead of react.

Day 108

Repair is Part of Responsibility

Sometimes responsibility means taking action after something has gone wrong. That action might look like apologizing, offering help, clarifying what happened, or making a different choice next time. Repair is not about erasing the mistake. It's about showing you care enough to clean it up.

What's a time when someone repaired something with you in a way that felt sincere? What did they do that made it feel real?

Just for this evening, I will remember that repair is a skill and not a performance.

Owning Your Impact ... Even If You Didn't Mean It

It's possible to have good intentions and still cause harm. That's not a character flaw. That's a human thing. The key is to listen when someone shares how your actions affected them and take that seriously, even if it wasn't what you meant.

What's one situation where you defended your intentions and missed the chance to listen to the impact? What would you do differently now?

Just for this evening, I will let the impact of my actions matter rather than just my intentions.

Day 110

Boundaries Can Be Part of Repair

Sometimes the most responsible thing you can do after a mistake is to set a boundary with yourself or with someone else. If you've hurt someone because you were stretched too thin, people-pleasing, or ignoring your limits, part of making it right might include saying no next time.

Where do you need to set a boundary so you don't keep repeating the same mistake?

Just for this evening, I will remember that boundaries are a form of responsibility.

Making It Right Doesn't Mean Fixing Everything

You can do your part to repair a situation, but that doesn't mean everything will go back to how it was. That's okay. Making things right is about taking ownership, not controlling the outcome. You don't need to be perfect. You just need to be honest and accountable.

Where have you avoided responsibility because you were afraid it wouldn't "fix" the situation?

Just for this evening, I will focus on doing what's mine to do and not on making everything perfect again.

Day 112

You're Allowed to Change

One of the best forms of repair is showing up differently next time. You don't need a dramatic declaration. Rather, you can show up with a new behavior that says, "I've learned something, and I care enough to try again." You don't have to be who you were before the mistake.

What's one way you've already changed because of a past mistake? How did that shift help you move forward?

Just for this evening, I will let my growth speak louder than my guilt.

You Can Apologize Without Over-Explaining

A strong apology doesn't need to come with a 20-minute explanation. Over-explaining often makes the other person feel like you're defending yourself more than you're hearing them. A powerful apology is clear, honest, and centered on the other person's experience.

Think of a time you received (or gave) an apology that felt too focused on excuses. What would have made it feel better?

Just for this evening, I will keep my apologies honest and not overworked.

Day 114

Letting Go After You've Done Your Part

After you've taken responsibility, made amends, and set healthy boundaries, the next step is letting go. You're not meant to live in permanent guilt. You are allowed to move forward. You've done your part. Now it's time to walk with your head up.

What's something you've been holding onto after you did what you could to make it right? What would it feel like to release it?

Just for this evening, I will carry the lesson and not the punishment.

You Are Not the Worst Thing You've Done
It's easy to take a moment, a mistake, a regret, or a decision and turn it into a label: selfish, careless, immature, toxic. You are not the worst thing you've done. You are a person learning through experience. You are not a walking mistake.

What label have you carried because of something you regret? What would it feel like to lay it down?

Just for this evening, I will see myself as more than my lowest moment.

Day 116

Shame Doesn't Make You More Accountable

Some people believe that staying ashamed will make them more responsible. Shame usually leads to hiding, freezing, or avoiding. Self-respect and honesty are better fuels for growth than self-hate ever will be.

Where in your life have you mistaken shame for maturity? What would accountability without shame look like instead?

Just for this evening, I will give myself room to grow instead of trapping myself in shame.

You're Allowed to Learn Out Loud

You don't have to disappear every time you make a mistake. Growth doesn't always happen in private, with perfect timing and hindsight. Sometimes you learn awkwardly, visibly, messily and in public. That doesn't make you weak. It makes you honest.

What would change if you stopped hiding every time you messed up and instead let yourself grow out loud?

Just for this evening, I will allow myself to be a work in progress in full view.

Day 118

You're Growing, Even When It's Quiet
Growth isn't always dramatic. Sometimes it's invisible, like pausing before reacting, asking a better question, or catching yourself mid-pattern. You might not get praise or closure, but that doesn't mean it's not happening. Quiet change still counts.

What's a quiet way you've grown recently that others might not notice, but you do?

Just for this evening, I will trust the value of the shifts happening quietly inside me.

Making Peace with the Past

Taking responsibility doesn't mean dragging your past behind you forever. It means looking back, learning what you can, and then choosing to move forward. You can make peace with the parts of your story that didn't go how you hoped. That doesn't get done by pretending they didn't happen but by deciding they don't get to define what happens next.

What's one decision, moment, or version of yourself you're ready to make peace with, not to erase it, but to release it?

Just for this evening, I will stop holding old mistakes like they're proof I don't deserve to grow.

Day 120

Who You Become by Owning It

Every time you take responsibility without spiraling into shame or hiding from yourself, you build something. You build trust, honesty, and inner strength. Owning your actions is about becoming someone you're proud to return to each night.

What's something you've done this since starting this chapter that you're proud of? What does it say about who you're becoming?

Just for this evening, I will let the way I show up for myself be part of who I am becoming.

How You Carry Responsibility Now

You started this chapter by exploring what responsibility meant to you. Maybe it felt heavy, scary, or full of pressure. Now you've learned that real responsibility is a relationship with yourself. It's how you build trust, grow with integrity, and walk forward without carrying shame.

What has shifted in your relationship with responsibility this over the last thirty days? How will you carry that into the next stage of your life?

Just for this evening, I will carry responsibility like a tool.

Give Yourself Credit

You've spent these last thirty-some days learning how to take responsibility in a new way that doesn't require shame or self-erasure. That's huge. It takes emotional strength to face your patterns, own your choices, and move forward without running from yourself.

What's something you've done this during the completion of this chapter (even something small) that you're proud of? What does it say about who you're becoming?

Just for this evening, I will give myself credit for the ways I've shown up and grown up.

Making and Managing Your Own Schedule

Time Is Yours Now

Your time is not just about productivity. It's about learning how to live without burning out or losing yourself. Adulthood gives you the power to decide how you spend your days. That freedom can feel both exciting and overwhelming. This chapter is about building a life that reflects your values, instead of everyone else's expectations.

What parts of your current schedule were created by you? What parts were inherited from school, family, or someone else's expectations?

Just for this evening, I will remember that I'm allowed to rebuild how I use my time.

Day 124

You're Not Lazy ... You're Probably Mismatched

So many new adults call themselves lazy when, really, they're just not working in sync with their energy. If you're trying to be a morning person but your brain doesn't turn on until noon, no planner will save you. Learning how you work best is the first step to any schedule that works at all.

When do you feel most awake, focused, or energized during the day? When do you crash?

Just for this evening, I will stop calling myself lazy for not working like someone else.

What Actually Matters to You?
You only get 24 hours per day. Some of that time goes to survival: eating, working, commuting. What about the rest? That's where your values show up. You need to know what matters enough to have it show up in your life.

What's one thing that really matters to you that hasn't been getting much of your time lately?

Just for this evening, I will give time to what makes my life feel meaningful.

Day 126

Your Schedule Is a Mirror
Your schedule already exists, even if it's messy. Look at your days. How much time goes to others? How much time goes to doomscrolling? How much time goes to rest? This isn't about judging yourself. It's about seeing clearly. Once you know where your time is actually going, you can begin to shift it.

If someone tracked your past three days, what would they say your priorities are? Do you agree with them?

Just for this evening, I will notice my patterns without punishing myself for them.

Planning for Energy, Not Just Tasks

Most planners treat time like a machine: block off an hour and get it done. However, you're not a machine. Some things take emotional energy. Some leave you drained. A schedule that works has to make space for the human that's following it.

What's one task that drains you more than it seems like it should? What could you do to support yourself before or after it?

Just for this evening, I will plan for the version of me that actually has to live the day.

Day 128

Identifying Your "Invisible" Time Sinks

Some parts of your day disappear without you even noticing. There's the 20-minute phone scroll that turns into an hour. There's the extra time you spend redoing something because you were exhausted when you first did it. These aren't moral failings, and noticing them is the first step to change.

What's something small that secretly eats up more of your time and energy than you expected?

Just for this evening, I will pay attention to where my time tends to vanish.

Your Time, Your Pace

Fast isn't always better. Packed doesn't always mean productive. Sometimes your natural pace is slower or more thoughtful or less structured. The point isn't to be like everyone else. It's to learn how you move through time.

If you could design your days at your natural rhythm, what would feel different from how things are now?

Just for this evening, I will let myself move at the pace that honors who I am.

Day 130

What You've Noticed So Far

You've spent the last several days observing your energy, your values, and your current relationship with time. This might've brought up frustration or clarity ... or maybe both. Either way, you're learning that owning your schedule starts with noticing. That's huge.

What's one thing you learned so far about how you actually use your time or energy? What do you want to do with that information?

Just for this evening, I will keep paying attention to my time, because awareness is the first change.

What Would a Supportive Schedule Look Like?

A supportive schedule doesn't just get things done. It also makes sure you don't fall apart in the process. It remembers that breaks are part of momentum and that rest is part of responsibility. It reflects that your needs matter as much as your tasks.

If your schedule was designed to support your well-being instead of just your output, what would it include more of?

Just for this evening, I will imagine a schedule where I'm protected and not just productive.

Day 132

Start With the Anchors

Trying to schedule everything can leave you overwhelmed before you begin. Instead, start with your anchors: sleep, meals, movement, work/school, and non-negotiables. Once you set those, the rest of the day has shape and space for freedom.

What are three non-negotiables you want to anchor your days around? (Think: sleep, meals, commitments, personal time, etc.)

Just for this evening, I will give structure to my day by choosing a few strong anchors.

Build Around Your Energy, Not Against It

You've already started noticing when your energy peaks and crashes. Now it's time to build around that. If you always feel fuzzy in the morning, why schedule your hardest task then? Give yourself the gift of working with your natural rhythm.

What's one part of your day you've been fighting against? What small shift could help it flow better?

Just for this evening, I will make space for my energy instead of ignoring it.

Day 134

Buffer Time Is Real Time

We tend to imagine we can jump from one thing to the next without breaks. Transitions need some energy, too. Commutes, mental resets, and snack runs all matter. Including buffer time isn't a flaw in your schedule. It's how you keep it honest.

Where are you consistently underestimating how long something takes? What would it feel like to finally build in room for it?

Just for this evening, I will treat buffer time as part of the plan.

Don't Schedule Every Minute

A schedule isn't a cage. It's a tool. You don't have to fill every hour to feel like you're in control. Too much structure can make you rebel or freeze. Leave breathing room. Let life … and you … breathe.

Where in your week could you leave intentional space just for being human?

Just for this evening, I will let my schedule include space to simply exist.

Day 136

Experiment. Don't Perfect.
The first version of your schedule doesn't have to be "the one." You're allowed to experiment, adjust, delete, and rebuild. You're not behind if you're still figuring it out. You're in process. That's what adulting looks like.

What part of your current schedule could you experiment with this week? The goal is not to fix it but rather to learn something about yourself?

Just for this evening, I will treat my schedule like a living thing and not a rigid rulebook.

Designing Around You
The most powerful thing about scheduling your own life is this: you get to build around who you are. You're not scheduling for who others expect you to be or who you "should" be by now. You're owning your time just for you.

If you believed your natural rhythm, values, and needs were valid, how would your schedule reflect that?

Just for this evening, I will remember that I'm the foundation my life is built on.

Day 138

Following Through Isn't About Perfection

You're not failing if you don't follow your schedule 100%. Life will shift. You will oversleep, run late, or forget something. The goal isn't perfect compliance. The goal is to show up more often than not, with grace. Following through means adjusting and continuing.

When you miss something on your schedule, how do you usually treat yourself? Do you need a kinder voice for yourself in those moments?

Just for this evening, I will give myself credit for showing up, not just finishing.

The Myth of "Catching Up"

Falling behind doesn't mean you have to sprint forward. "Catching up" often leads to burnout. Instead, pick up from where you are. One missed day doesn't mean the whole week is ruined. You're allowed to re-enter gently.

What's one area of your schedule where you could restart instead of trying to catch up all at once?

Just for this evening, I will meet myself where I am, instead of where I think I should be.

Day 140

Build Momentum, Not Pressure

Small wins compound. When you check off something tiny from your to-do list, your brain releases a little dose of motivation. That's momentum. Trying to power through everything at once kills that. Build your schedule around small steps that add up and not just big moves.

What's one small thing you can check off tomorrow that would build a sense of momentum?

Just for this evening, I will treat small steps as success, rather than warm-ups.

Routines Help When Motivation Doesn't

You won't feel motivated every day. That's normal. Routines carry you when motivation flakes out. If you brush your teeth without thinking, you can eventually do the same with writing, planning, or showing up to class. Build habits that don't rely on your mood.

What's one routine you could start tying to something you already do, like meals, waking up, or winding down?

Just for this evening, I will build on what's already working instead of starting from scratch.

Day 142

Self-Talk Is a Tool. It's Not a Threat.

If your inner voice is constantly yelling "DO BETTER," your schedule will start to feel like punishment. That voice doesn't make you more productive. It just makes you more anxious. Speak to yourself like someone who wants you to succeed.

What do you need your inner voice to say tomorrow, when things don't go as planned?

Just for this evening, I will practice being on my own team.

Respect Beats Discipline
Discipline has a reputation for being cold and rigid. Meanwhile, real follow-through comes from respect for your energy, your values, and your time. You're more likely to keep a schedule when it reflects what matters and not just what's urgent.

What's one part of your schedule that reflects your values? How can you honor it more deeply this week?

Just for this evening, I will follow through because I respect myself and not because I fear failure.

Day 144

When You Want to Quit, Pause Instead

You'll want to give up some days. You'll feel like none of it matters. That's fatigue talking. You don't have to quit. You just need to pause. A break can save you from burnout. A breath can save your momentum. Rest is not the end.

When you feel like giving up on a plan, what could a pause look like instead?

Just for this evening, I will choose pause over quit.

Rigid Plans Crack Under Pressure

The tighter you grip your schedule, the more it breaks when life happens. And life will happen. There will be sick days, missed buses, and changed minds. Flexibility is a necessary skill. It's adaptation. A good schedule bends. A good life requires it.

What's one time your plan got derailed recently? How did you respond to it?

Just for this evening, I will allow my schedule to flex without crumbling.

Day 146

Everything Doesn't Have to Move
When one part of your schedule shifts, the whole day doesn't have to collapse. You don't have to scrap the whole day to make one adjustment.

What's one anchor in your schedule you can return to when things go off track?

Just for this evening, I will let one setback just stay small.

Rewriting Is a Skill ... Not a Setback

Changing your schedule isn't admitting failure. It's showing maturity. You're allowed to re-prioritize when new things come up. The point isn't to never rewrite your plans. The point is to know how to rewrite with clarity instead of chaos.

`What's one thing on your to-do list that may need to be renegotiated this week?

Just for this evening, I will treat change as a choice rather than as a collapse.

Day 148

Plan B Is Still a Plan

It's easy to think backup plans are somehow less real. Yet, they can be the reason you stay grounded. Flexibility means having options. It doesn't mean your abandoning your structure. When Plan A falls through, Plan B keeps you steady.

What's one area of your life where you could prepare a soft backup just in case?

Just for this evening, I will give myself options without guilt

.

Being Kind to the Version of You Who Has to Show Up

Some days you'll be tired, stressed, distracted, or sad. That version of you still has to live the day. A flexible schedule lets that version of you have a chance. Your future self will thank you for making space for those needs.

What's one thing you could build into your schedule this week to support your more vulnerable moments?

Just for this evening, I will schedule with compassion.

Day 150

Control Isn't the Goal

The goal of a schedule isn't to control every outcome. It's to give you agency. Control says, "Nothing can go wrong." Agency instead says, "even if it does go wrong, I have a way forward." You can't control the world, but you can build tools to move through it.

What's one moment today where you felt in control? What's one moment from today where you had agency, even if things weren't perfect?

Just for this evening, I will trade control for something stronger: agency.

Flexibility Doesn't Mean Saying Yes to Everything

Being flexible isn't the same as being endlessly available. It's not your job to bend for every request, deadline, or crisis. Flexibility is intentional. It's the difference between being adaptable and being a doormat. You can be both responsive and boundaried.

Where in your life does "being flexible" actually look more like people-pleasing? How could you shift that?

Just for this evening, I will stretch, but I won't snap.

Day 152

Change Is Not the Enemy of Structure

Many people abandon planning altogether because "things always change anyway." Flexibility and structure are not opposites. They're partners. A strong schedule leaves space for life to happen. When you expect change, you're not thrown by it. Instead, you're ready for it.

What's one way you could build "wiggle room" into your week, instead of pretending things will always go as planned?

Just for this evening, I will build space for change, not fight it.

Your Schedule, Your Terms

This chapter has been about more than just time management. It's been about reclaiming your time, your energy, and your rhythm. You've learned to listen to yourself, to build around your truth, and to stay grounded even when things shift. That's adulting, and you're doing it.

What part of your relationship with time or structure has changed the most over the last thirty or so days?

Just for this evening, I will carry forward the version of me who knows how to choose.

Setting and Keeping Boundaries

You're Allowed to Take Up Space

This chapter is about learning how to protect your energy, time, and emotional well-being. This is done not by building walls, but by drawing lines that let the right things in and keep the harmful stuff out. Boundaries aren't selfish. They're how you stay whole.

You've probably been told, directly or indirectly, to shrink. You've been told to say, "yes" when you wanted to say, "no." You've been told to be agreeable, flexible, and helpful. While those things aren't bad on their own, they become harmful when they erase you. This chapter is about boundaries. You'll be learning to set boundaries, not to push others away, but to make space for your full self. You are not too much. You are not selfish. You're allowed to take up space.

What's one time you said "yes" when you really wanted to say "no?" What would it have felt like to say no?

Just for this evening, I will remind myself that taking up space isn't rude.

Day 155

Boundaries Are About You, Not Controlling Others

A boundary is not a rule for someone else. It's a limit you set for yourself. You can't control someone else's behavior, but you can control what you allow, what you respond to, and what you walk away from. Boundaries are the bridge between your values and your actions.

What's one situation in your life where you've been trying to change someone else instead of setting a clear limit for yourself?

Just for this evening, I will focus on what I can control: my actions and not someone else's.

Being "Nice" Isn't the Same as Being Kind

We're often raised to be "nice." In other words, we're told by "the grown-ups" to be agreeable, polite, and accommodating. Kindness isn't the same thing. Kindness is honest. Kindness includes yourself. If you're always putting others first to keep the peace, ask yourself: whose peace is it, really?

Where in your life have you confused being nice with being kind? How would it feel to include yourself in your kindness?

Just for this evening, I will practice kindness that doesn't erase me.

Day 157

Boundaries Create Safety, Not Distance
Healthy boundaries don't build walls. They build trust. When people know what to expect from you, relationships become clearer and safer. Boundaries aren't rejection. They're a form of respect for yourself and for others.

What's one relationship in your life that would benefit from clearer expectations or limits?

Just for this evening, I will remember that clarity is a kindness.

Discomfort Isn't the Same as Danger

Setting boundaries can feel really uncomfortable, especially if you're used to going along with things to avoid conflict. That discomfort doesn't mean you're doing something wrong. It means you're growing. You can survive someone else's disappointment. You're not in danger. You're just doing something new.

What's one boundary you've avoided setting because you didn't want to feel uncomfortable?

Just for this evening, I will let growth be uncomfortable and not view it as unsafe.

Day 159

Saying No Doesn't Make You Mean

"No" is not a bad word. It's a full sentence. When you say no, you're not being difficult. You're being honest. You're honoring your time, energy, and capacity. That's not mean. That's mature.

What's one thing you want to say "no" to this week. What would saying "no" make room for?

Just for this evening, I will treat "no" as an act of self-trust.

You Don't Have to Earn Rest

One of the most overlooked boundaries is rest. You don't have to be exhausted to deserve a break. You don't have to prove your productivity to justify stillness. Rest is a right. Rest is not a reward. Boundaries help protect that.

When do you find yourself waiting until you're "done" to allow rest? How could you build rest into your routine sooner?

Just for this evening, I will protect my rest like it matters … because it does.

Day 161

Your Needs Are Not Inconvenient
Many of us grow up thinking our needs are a burden. If we speak up, we'll be seen as difficult or too much. However, needing rest, space, respect, clarity, or support isn't unreasonable. It's human. Learning to recognize and honor your needs is one of the most adult things you can do.

Where in your life have you minimized your needs to make things easier for someone else?

Just for this evening, I will remind myself that I am not an inconvenience.

Naming What You Need is the First Step

You can't meet a need you can't name. It's easy to say, "I'm just tired" or "I feel off." There's power in pausing and asking, "what do I really need right now?" Maybe it's reassurance. Maybe it's quiet. Maybe it's help. The more precisely you name it, the better chance you have of meeting it.

What is one unmet need you've been feeling lately, and how could you name it more clearly?

Just for this evening, I will practice asking myself, "What do I need right now?"

Day 163

It's Okay to Need Different Things Than Other People

You don't need to justify your needs by proving someone else has the same ones. What works for your friend, your parent, or your partner might not work for you. That doesn't make you wrong. It makes you self-aware. Comparison is not a substitute for clarity.

Where have you doubted yourself just because your needs were different from the people around you?

Just for this evening, I will let go of the need to match someone else's map.

Boundaries Can Be Temporary

Sometimes a boundary is forever. Sometimes it's for this season, this semester, or this week. You're allowed to set limits based on where you are right now emotionally, physically, and financially. You don't need to promise permanence to give yourself permission.

Is there a limit you need to set right now that doesn't have to be permanent?

Just for this evening, I will trust myself to revisit boundaries as I grow.

Day 165

Meeting Your Needs Helps You Show Up Better for Others
When you meet your own needs, you become more grounded and more generous. You're not running on fumes or resentment. You're coming from a place of choice. Boundaries don't push people away, but unmet needs do.

How does tending to your own needs actually help your relationships?

Just for this evening, I will let self-care be a way of showing up better for others.

Needing Help Doesn't Make You Weak
Asking for help can feel like a weakness. Needing support is not a flaw. It's part of being alive. Strong people know when they're not meant to carry things alone. Boundaries sometimes mean letting others in.

What's one thing you've been struggling with that you haven't asked for help with and why?

Just for this evening, I will remember that reaching out can be a strength.

Day 167

You Don't Owe Everyone an Explanation
You're allowed to say no without a 10-minute "TED Talk" justifying it. Boundaries don't require a detailed defense. They require clarity. When you over-explain, you risk talking yourself out of your own limits. Trust that your "no" can stand on its own.

When have you given an explanation just to soften a boundary? How did it make you feel?

Just for this evening, I will practice short, clear statements that honor my truth.

Guilt Is Not a Sign You're Doing Something Wrong

If setting boundaries feels wrong, it's often because you've been taught that pleasing others matters more than protecting yourself. Guilt shows up not because you're being bad, but because you're doing something different. Let that guilt be a growth signpost, not a stop sign.

What's one boundary that makes you feel guilty? What might that guilt be trying to teach you?

Just for this evening, I will let guilt pass through without letting it drive.

Day 169

Use Language That Centers You

Good boundaries aren't about blaming the other person. They're about expressing what you will or won't do. They rest on "I" statements instead of "you" statements: "I need…", "I'm not available…", "I've decided…" This isn't selfish. It's self-accountability. You're not labeling someone else as wrong. You're owning your own limits.

Try rewriting a recent confrontation using "I" statements instead of blame. How does it shift the tone?

Just for this evening, I will speak from my truth, not from their behavior.

Practice Ahead of Time

You don't have to wait for a stressful moment to figure out what to say. Practicing boundary language when you're calm makes it easier to access when you're nervous. Write it down. Say it in the mirror. Try it with a trusted friend. Your voice gets stronger with use.

What's one boundary you've been avoiding? How could you rehearse saying it aloud?

Just for this evening, I will prepare in order to stay calm and not panic.

Day 171

It's Not Your Job to Manage Other People's Reactions

When you set a boundary, someone might get upset. That doesn't mean you were wrong to set it. Their feelings are valid and still not your responsibility to fix. You can be compassionate without abandoning yourself.

What's one time you didn't set a boundary because you feared someone's reaction?

Just for this evening, I will let people feel what they feel without making it my burden.

You Can Be Direct and Caring
Clarity is kindness. You don't have to be cold to be clear. You don't have to be harsh to be honest. The best boundaries come from a place of self-respect and respect for others. You can say what you mean with heart.

What does "direct and caring" look like in your tone, your words, and your body language?

Just for this evening, I will speak with both backbone and warmth.

Day 173

It's OK That Not Everyone Will Like Your Boundaries
When you start setting boundaries, not everyone will cheer you on. Some people might feel confused, hurt, or frustrated. This may be especially so if they benefited from you not having boundaries before. That doesn't mean you're wrong. It means the dynamic is changing, and change can feel threatening to those who relied on your silence.

Think of someone who's reacted poorly when you set a limit. What do you think they were really reacting to?

Just for this evening, I will allow others to feel discomfort without shrinking to make them more comfortable.

You Don't Have to Argue Your Boundary

It's tempting to get pulled into a debate when someone challenges your boundary. A boundary is not a discussion. It's a decision. You can be calm, clear, and kind … and still say, "this is what I need." No follow-up required.

What boundary have you felt the need to "defend" or "prove?" What would it feel like to simply hold it instead?

Just for this evening, I will let my clarity be enough.

Day 175

Broken Boundaries Deserve Consequences, Not Just Warnings
A boundary without a consequence is just a preference. If someone repeatedly crosses your limit, it's not unkind to follow through. It's necessary. You don't need to raise your voice or make threats. Quiet consistency is powerful. It's how trust is built … or rebuilt.

What boundary in your life needs a clearer follow-through?

ust for this evening, I will follow my limits with action, not just words.

"No" is a Complete Sentence, And So is "I'm Leaving"

Sometimes boundaries mean walking away from a conversation, a group, or a relationship. That doesn't make you dramatic or fragile. It means you've honored your limit, and someone else hasn't. You get to remove yourself without apology.

Have you ever stayed in a situation longer than you should have because you felt bad leaving?

Just for this evening, I will let peace be a good enough reason to walk away.

Day 177

You Can Rebuild Boundaries That Got Blurry
It's okay if a boundary you set once has gotten messy or unclear. Life changes, relationships evolve, and your energy shifts. You're allowed to re-clarify, reassert, or reset your boundaries at any time.

What's one boundary that used to feel clear, but has gotten blurry lately?

Just for this evening, I will give myself permission to start again.

Sometimes the Hardest Boundary Is the One You Set with Someone You Love

Boundaries aren't just for people who mistreat you. Sometimes they're most needed with the people you care about deeply. Sometimes they're most needed with the ones who drain you without realizing it or ask too much because they love you. Boundaries with love are still love. They help love last.

Is there someone you care about who you've avoided setting boundaries with? What would one honest boundary look like?

Just for this evening, I will remember that love and limits can exist together.

Day 179

Show Up for Yourself to Sow Self-Respect

It's easy to think of boundaries as something we set for other people. Some of the most important ones are the quiet promises we keep to ourselves. Showing up when you say you will. Sticking to your budget. Logging off when you're overstimulated. Self-boundaries aren't punishment. They're protection for your future self.

What's one small commitment to yourself that you often break? How would it feel to keep it?

Just for this evening, I will treat my own time and energy like it matters.

Know the Difference Between Flexibility and Self-Betrayal
Life is unpredictable. Sometimes plans change, and being able to bend is healthy. However, if you constantly move your own goalposts, especially to please others, you risk losing trust in yourself. Flexibility is wise. Self-betrayal is exhausting.

Where have you been too quick to give yourself a pass? What's the impact?

Just for this evening, I will make room for grace instead of excuses.

Day 181

Your Body Sets Boundaries, Too

Your body gives you signs when you've pushed too far: a racing heart, tight shoulders, or sudden exhaustion. When you've spent years ignoring those signals, it can take time to tune back in. Somatic boundaries (like rest, space, hydration) matter just as much as emotional ones.

What is your body trying to tell you lately? How can you honor it?

Just for this evening, I will listen to what my body needs and not just what my calendar says.

Be Honest About What You Can Handle

Overcommitting is a form of self-abandonment. It might look like ambition or helpfulness. If you're constantly running on empty, something has to give. Protecting your capacity isn't laziness. It's sustainability. You don't have to prove anything by burning out.

What's one thing you've said "yes" to lately that you didn't actually have capacity for?

Just for this evening, I will value my bandwidth like a limited resource.

Day 183

Forgive Yourself for the Times You Didn't Hold the Line

There will be times you abandon your own boundaries. Sometimes this is out of fear, out of pressure, or out of habit. That's part of learning. Shame says, "you'll never get it right." Growth says, "start again." The boundary still belongs to you, and so does the choice to return to it.

Think of a recent time you slipped on a personal boundary. What did you learn, and what do you want to try next time?

Just for this evening, I will choose curiosity and beginning again over shame.

What Respect Feels Like

With this chapter, you've practiced seeing boundaries not as walls, but as invitations to deeper respect, greater clarity, and real connection. You've learned that saying "no" doesn't make you cold, and saying "yes" to yourself isn't selfish. You've drawn lines that protect your peace, and that's something to be proud of. Boundaries aren't just about others. They're about choosing a life where you show up whole.

What has changed in the way you think about boundaries with others and with yourself?

Just for this evening, I will honor the space I need, the voice I have, and the person I'm becoming.

Handling Criticism and Feedback

What Criticism Feels Like

Nobody loves being criticized, especially when you're just starting out in the world and trying to figure out who you are. Criticism can feel personal, sharp, and even humiliating. It's also part of adult life. Learning how to deal with it without spiraling is a powerful skill. In this chapter, we'll explore how to tell the difference between helpful and harmful feedback, how to hold on to your worth, and how to grow from what's true.

When was the last time criticism really stung? What did it bring up for you emotionally?

Just for this evening, I will stay open to learning, even when it's uncomfortable.

Day 186

Criticism Feels Personal Even When It Isn't

When someone criticizes something you've done, it often feels like they're criticizing who you are. That's a normal reaction. Your brain is wired to perceive rejection as danger. Not all feedback is an attack. Some of it is data, and all of it is survivable.

Think about a time you got defensive. Was it about the content of the feedback or the feeling that you were being judged?

Just for this evening, I will pause before reacting to ask, "Is this about me as a person, or something I did?"

Not All Criticism Is Created Equal

There's a huge difference between thoughtful feedback and someone just being mean. Helpful criticism focuses on actions and outcomes. Harmful criticism goes after your character or intentions. You're allowed to learn from one and ignore the other.

Can you remember feedback that helped you improve and feedback that just hurt? What was the difference?

Just for this evening, I will learn to tell the difference between helpful and harmful voices

Day 188

People Give Feedback Through Their Own Lens
Someone's criticism often reveals more about them than about you. Their standards, experiences, insecurities, and values all shape how they respond. That doesn't mean their feedback is wrong, but it does mean you don't have to take it as absolute truth.

Have you ever gotten feedback that clashed with who you want to be? How did you decide what to keep and what to release?

Just for this evening, I will remember that one person's opinion isn't the whole story.

Some Criticism is About Control, Not Care

Sometimes people use criticism to try to shrink or shame you instead of help you grow. That's not feedback. That's control. You don't owe everyone access to your energy, especially if they consistently make you feel small.

Who do you struggle to take feedback from? Is it because they want to help, or because they want to dominate?

Just for this evening, I will protect my self-worth from those who don't deserve to shape it.

Day 190

The Delivery Matters ... But So Does the Content

Even well-meaning people can give clumsy or harsh feedback. Even rude people can sometimes offer something true. It's okay to separate how something is said from what is being said. You can be gracious and still set boundaries for future conversations.

Has anyone ever said something that was true, but in a hurtful way? What did you take from it and what did you leave behind?

Just for this evening, I will choose what I carry forward

You're Allowed to Ask for Feedback Differently

If criticism tends to derail you, you can make a plan for how you want to receive it. You can ask someone to email it instead of bringing it up in front of others. You can ask for specific feedback instead of vague critique. Advocating for how you learn best is a sign of maturity and not weakness.

What would it look like to set some ground rules for how you prefer to receive feedback?

Just for this evening, I will shape my learning environment with intention.

Day 192

The First Reaction is Usually Defensive
Your first reaction to criticism is usually about protection and not truth. When your brain senses threat, it looks for ways to defend, shut down, or push back. Growth begins when you create a small pause between what you hear and how you respond.

What's your typical first response to feedback? How long does it take you to move into a more grounded place?

Just for this evening, I will give myself permission to pause instead of defend.

You Don't Have to Agree in the Moment
You can hear someone's feedback without immediately agreeing, disagreeing, or reacting at all. "Thanks for the feedback … I'll think about it," is a full sentence. Learning to sit with feedback before judging it helps you respond instead of react.

What's one time you wish you had waited before responding to feedback?

Just for this evening, I will let feedback land before I decide what to do with it

Day 194

Curiosity is a Superpower

When you shift from "how dare they say that" to "I wonder why they said that," everything changes. Curiosity pulls you out of shame and into learning. It helps you zoom out and see patterns, intentions, and even truths you may have missed.

Can you think of feedback that stung but made more sense once you got curious about it?

Just for this evening, I will ask, "What might this be showing me?"

You Can Separate Tone from Truth

Some people give feedback with a harsh tone, and it's tempting to write them off completely. Sometimes there's still truth underneath their delivery. Practicing the skill of emotional separation (hearing what's helpful without absorbing the venom) keeps you in your power.

Have you ever received feedback that was poorly delivered but still valuable?

Just for this evening, I will look for the gold, even if it's buried.

Day 196

Your Worth is Not on Trial
Getting feedback doesn't mean you've failed. It means you're growing. Your worth isn't something that rises or falls based on someone's opinion. You're not being graded. You're being guided. You're allowed to hold that with dignity.

What feedback have you taken as a personal indictment instead of an invitation to grow?

Just for this evening, I will hold feedback in one hand and my self-worth in the other.

It's Okay to Be Hurt and Still Learn

Sometimes feedback does hurt. That doesn't mean you're being overly sensitive or immature. It means you care. Growth doesn't require you to numb out. You can feel the sting and still choose to explore what's useful. You're allowed to do both.

What's one piece of feedback that hurt but helped you change for the better?

Just for this evening, I will let pain be a teacher rather than a wall.

Day 198

Practice Makes Feedback Easier

Handling criticism is a skill. Like any skill, it gets easier with practice. The more feedback you get, the more familiar it becomes. With time, you'll start to see it less as a threat and more as a resource for growth. You don't have to love it. You just have to learn from it.

How has your ability to receive feedback changed over the last year or two?

Just for this evening, I will treat feedback as part of the process, not the end of the story.

Not All Feedback Needs Immediate Action

Not every piece of feedback requires an instant response or change. You are allowed to think, reflect, and move at your own pace instead of reacting quickly. Real growth happens when you give yourself time to decide what truly fits.

What's one piece of feedback you've felt pressured to act on quickly? What might happen if you slowed it down?

Just for this evening, I will remember that reflection is productive, too.

Day 200

Patterns Matter More Than Outliers

One person's opinion is a data point. Multiple people saying the same thing? That's a pattern. Growth is easier when you focus on repeated signals, not random noise. You don't need to change every time someone criticizes you, but you can take patterns seriously.

What feedback have you heard more than once and what might it be pointing to?

Just for this evening, I will pay more attention to echoes than to outbursts.

Growth Doesn't Mean Agreeing with Everything

You can grow from feedback without completely agreeing with it. Sometimes the value is in the reflection it sparks, not in the conclusion you reach. Maturity means being able to say, "I've thought about this and here's what I've decided."

When have you grown from feedback even though you didn't fully agree with it?

Just for this evening, I will allow feedback to guide me instead of override me.

Day 202

You Can Try Things On Without Committing

Think of feedback like a jacket. You don't have to wear it forever. You can just try it on and see how it fits. Experimenting with new behaviors or perspectives can teach you more than arguing about them. You get to test things before you decide they're part of you.

What's one piece of feedback you could "try on" this week, just to see how it feels?

Just for this evening, I will experiment without pressure.

Your Strengths Can Be Double-Edged

Some feedback doesn't mean "change this." It means "balance this." A strength, like being honest, driven, or helpful, can become a weakness if it's overused. Learning to calibrate your strengths is a powerful form of growth.

What strength of yours might sometimes go too far? What would a healthy balance look like?

Just for this evening, I will tune my strengths and not mute them.

Day 204

Feedback is a Gift That You Choose Whether to Open It
It's okay to say, "thank you" and later decide, "this isn't for me." You're the gatekeeper of what enters your self-image. When you treat feedback like an offering, not an order, you stay in charge of your own story.

What's one piece of feedback you've been holding but maybe don't need to keep?

Just for this evening, I will keep what fits and leave what doesn't.

Growth Is a Lifelong Process
There's no finish line when it comes to personal growth. You're allowed to be a work in progress. You're allowed to change your mind about what works for you. Feedback isn't a one-time fix. It's an invitation to evolve … again and again.

What's something you've learned recently that you wouldn't have been ready to hear a year ago?

Just for this evening, I will meet myself where I am and stay open to what's next.

Day 206

Feedback Is a Form of Care
Feedback, when given with care, is a sign that someone believes in your growth. If you didn't matter, there would be no reason to offer guidance or honesty. Giving feedback is a way of saying you see someone's potential and want to support it.

What makes you more likely to accept feedback from someone and how can you model that when giving it?

Just for this evening, I will give feedback from a place of belief rather than blame.

Start With Relationship, Rather Than Correction

People are more likely to hear your feedback when they know you care. Building trust first through kindness, respect, and presence gives your words a stronger foundation. Without that, even gentle feedback can land like criticism.

Who do you feel safe receiving feedback from? What makes their voice easier to hear?

Just for this evening, I will remember that trust speaks louder than critique.

Day 208

Be Specific, Not Vague

"Do better" isn't feedback. Here's what is clear feedback: "I noticed you interrupted three times during the meeting … maybe try letting people finish their thought." Clear feedback points to behaviors instead of personalities and gives the person something they can actually work on.

Have you ever been confused by feedback that wasn't specific? How could it have been clearer?

Just for this evening, I will focus on what someone did and not who they are.

Watch Your Tone ... It Carries More Than You Think

People don't just hear what you say. They feel how you say it. Tone, body language, and even timing matter. You don't have to sugarcoat, but you do have to be responsible for your delivery. Respect doesn't weaken your message. It strengthens it.

How do you think your tone affects how your feedback is received?

Just for this evening, I will speak in a way that makes it easier to be heard.

Day 210

Ask Before You Offer

Not everyone is ready for feedback, and that's okay. It gives people agency to ask, "would you like some thoughts?" or "are you open to feedback?" It builds trust. Consent matters in emotional conversations, too.

How do you respond when someone offers unsolicited advice? How might asking change that?

Just for this evening, I will honor people's readiness before I speak.

Leave Room for Growth, Not Guilt

The goal of feedback isn't to make someone feel bad. It's to help them move forward. The best feedback leaves someone feeling clear, encouraged, and empowered to change. That doesn't mean it won't sting, but it should always offer a way through.

What kind of feedback leaves you feeling hopeful instead of ashamed?

Just for this evening, I will speak to what's possible and not just what's wrong.

Day 212

You're Allowed to Keep Evolving
Learning how to handle criticism and feedback is one of the most powerful emotional skills you'll ever develop. It helps you protect your peace, grow with intention, and speak to others with courage and care. You don't have to get it perfect. You just have to keep practicing. You're allowed to mess up, try again, and evolve your voice over time.

What's one piece of feedback (given or received) that changed you in a meaningful way?

Just for this evening, I will keep learning how to listen and speak with both honesty and heart.

Leap Year

Surprise! You knew it had to be in here somewhere ...
It's a day that only comes around once every four years. It's like a hidden pocket in the calendar and a secret day tucked between the pages. It's the perfect time to imagine your life four years from now. It's a great time ponder not just where you might be, but who you want to become.

You've already spent time showing up for yourself in this journal. You've been reflecting, learning, and maybe stumbling. Where does all of this lead?

This isn't about five-year plans or perfectly mapped-out futures. It's about setting a soft, curious vision for your next Leap Year self. The version of you who will wake up on February 29, 2028 and think, "Wow, look how far I've come!"

Picture yourself four years from today.
You're four years older. Maybe you're in a new city, a new job, a new relationship, or maybe not. Where do you hope to be emotionally, mentally, physically, and spiritually? What will you be great at that you're just beginning to learn now? What parts of you do you hope will stay the same? What parts are you ready to outgrow?

Just for this evening, I will take one small step tonight that Future Me will thank me for ... even if it's just imagining what's possible.

Practicing Self-Compassion When You Screw Up

What If You Didn't Have to Be So Hard on Yourself?

You don't have to be cruel to yourself in order to grow. This chapter is about practicing real self-compassion, especially when you mess up or feel like you don't deserve it. Taking responsibility doesn't require self-destruction. It requires kindness, honesty, and the courage to try again.

When you think about being kinder to yourself, what worries come up? What are you afraid might happen if you stop being so hard on yourself?

Just for this evening, I will open the door just a little to the idea that being gentler with myself might actually help me grow.

Day 214

The Inner Critic Isn't the Whole Truth

Most people have a running commentary in their heads. A lot of the time, that voice isn't very nice. It might sound like your own voice, but it's often an echo of people who were once critical, disappointed, or demanding. That voice might be loud, but that doesn't mean it's right. The first step toward self-compassion is realizing: you are not your thoughts.

What's something your inner voice says to you when you make a mistake? Where do you think that voice came from?

Just for this evening, I will notice the voice in my head and question whether it's telling the truth.

Self-Compassion ≠ Excusing Everything
A lot of people think that being kind to yourself means making excuses. That's not compassion. That's avoidance. Real self-compassion is saying, "I messed up, but I'm still worthy of love and growth." You can hold yourself accountable without tearing yourself apart. In fact, you're more likely to change when you feel safe to try again.

Have you ever confused self-compassion with being "too easy" on yourself?

Just for this evening, I will remember that self-compassion supports change.

Day 216

Would You Say That to a Friend?

One of the simplest tools in self-compassion is this: when your inner voice gets cruel, ask yourself, "would I say this to someone I care about?" Most of the time, the answer is no. So why do we speak to ourselves in ways we'd never speak to a friend? That inner cruelty isn't strength. It's just hurt, wearing armor.

Write down a recent self-criticism. Now rephrase it the way you'd say it to a close friend.

Just for this evening, I will speak to myself like someone who matters.

You Can Feel Shame Without Becoming It
Shame is sneaky. It tells you that you are your worst moment. Clearly, that's not true. Feeling bad about what you've done can be healthy. It means you care. Becoming consumed by that feeling doesn't help you grow. Naming the emotion ("this is shame") is the first way to loosen its grip.

What's a moment you've felt shame over? How could you speak to that part of yourself with more compassion?

Just for this evening, I will remind myself: "This is a feeling. It's not my identity."

Day 218

You Get to Choose a Kinder Voice
The voice in your head isn't fixed. It's trainable. You can learn to speak to yourself with honesty and warmth. It takes practice, like learning a new language. Every time you interrupt the cruel voice and replace it with a gentler one, you're creating a new pattern. The new pattern says, "I deserve to be treated with care."

What might a compassionate inner voice say to you tonight?

Just for this evening, I will try out a kinder tone, even if it feels unfamiliar.

Emotional Pain Is Not a Disqualification

Emotional pain does not make you broken or unworthy of care. Feeling deeply is not a failure, it is a sign that you are alive and capable of growth. Your pain doesn't disqualify you from love, healing, or becoming who you're meant to be.

When you're hurting, what do you tend to tell yourself? What would it look like to tell a different story?

Just for this evening, I will let myself be both hurting and healing.

Day 220

You Don't Have to Vanish to Be Safe

A lot of us learned that the best way to survive criticism or failure was to disappear emotionally, socially, or even physically. We ghost friends. We cancel plans. We bury ourselves in distractions. Disappearing doesn't heal us. What if staying in your body, in your life, or in your relationships could be safer than you thought?

When was the last time you emotionally "checked out" after something hard? What might help you stay present next time?

Just for this evening, I will stay with myself, even when I feel the urge to hide.

Numbing Is a Signal ... Not a Solution
When the pain gets too big, numbing can feel like relief. Scrolling, binge-watching, overworking, or overeating is all so understandable. Numbing doesn't make the pain go away. It just puts it on mute. When the volume comes back up, it's often louder. Instead of judging your coping, try to listen to it. What is it trying to protect you from?

What's one way you tend to numb yourself when you're overwhelmed? What might you try instead, even for 5 minutes?

Just for this evening, I will notice when I want to numb and gently ask myself why.

Day 222

You Can Ask for Comfort Without Explaining Everything
Sometimes we don't reach out because we think we have to explain or justify our pain. You don't need to have the "right words" to deserve support. Saying, "I'm not okay right now ... can we just be in the same room?" or "can you remind me that I'm not a bad person?" is enough. You don't have to perform your pain to be cared for.

Who in your life might be a safe person to ask for comfort, even without giving them the full story?

Just for this evening, I will remind myself: "I don't need to be perfectly articulate to deserve connection."

Hiding Your Hurt Doesn't Make You Stronger

We're taught that being "low-maintenance" is admirable and that needing less, feeling less, expressing less makes us more lovable. Hiding your hurt doesn't make you strong. It just makes you alone. Real strength is saying, "I'm not okay, and I'm still worthy of love." You're worthy of love even in the mess. You're worthy love even when you're not sure how to explain.

What messages did you grow up with about showing emotion or vulnerability?

Just for this evening, I will let myself be seen.

Day 224

Pain Is a Tunnel
When you're in pain, it can feel like you'll never get through it. It can feel like you're trapped. Pain is not a permanent place. It's a tunnel. And, the only way out of a tunnel is to go through it. The good news is you don't have to rush it. You don't have to sprint. You just have to keep moving, even slowly.

Think of a time you moved through something difficult. What helped you keep going?

Just for this evening, I will take one breath and one step and that's enough for today.

You Don't Have to Earn Forgiveness with Punishment

You don't have to be perfect or suffer in order to be allowed to move forward. Punishing yourself doesn't make you more deserving of healing or forgiveness. Real growth comes from understanding, repair, and choosing compassion instead of shame.

When have you believed that punishing yourself was the right or necessary thing to do? What else might have helped instead?

Just for this evening, I will stop keeping score between my pain and my worth.

Day 226

Repair Doesn't Require Perfection

You might think that you have to say the perfect thing, do the perfect thing, or be perfectly changed before you're allowed to make amends or begin again. People don't need your perfection. They need your sincerity. They need your willingness to take responsibility and keep showing up. You can start repairing even while you're still learning.

Is there a relationship or situation where you've been waiting to be "ready" before trying to make things better?

Just for this evening, I will allow myself to begin the repair process, even if it's imperfect.

Forward Is a Direction, Not a Speed
When you're trying to move on from something, especially a mistake, it's easy to get discouraged if you don't feel like you're "over it" fast enough. Healing and progress aren't races. Sometimes forward looks like baby steps. Sometimes it looks like pausing. The important thing is that you're not staying stuck.

What's one way you've made forward progress recently, even if it felt small?

Just for this evening, I will honor my pace, instead of punish it.

Day 228

You Can Grow in the Middle of the Mess

You don't have to wait until your life is all cleaned up to be growing. In fact, growth often happens in the mess ... not after it. It happens when you admit something isn't working. When you say the hard thing. When you show up even though you feel like a disaster. You're not disqualified from growth because you're still figuring things out.

What part of your life feels messy right now? How might growth still be happening there?

Just for this evening, I will let myself be a work in progress and a person of value.

You're Allowed to Feel Proud, Even if You're Not Finished
Some people think pride is only allowed when you've fully succeeded. There's another kind of pride. It's the kind that comes from effort, intention, and resilience. You can be proud of showing up and proud of trying again. You can be proud of growing in private. You don't have to wait until the end of the story to celebrate the progress you've made.

What is something you've done recently that you haven't let yourself be proud of but deserve to?

Just for this evening, I will allow myself a small moment of pride. I've earned it.

Day 230

You Can Move Forward Without All the Answers

It's okay if you don't have it all figured out. Moving forward doesn't require a perfect plan. It requires willingness. It requires willingness to try, to risk being wrong, and to choose again tomorrow. Life is rarely made of big, confident leaps. It's made of small, hopeful steps in the right direction, even when the destination isn't clear yet.

What's something you could do tomorrow that would move you even a little closer to peace or clarity?

Just for this evening, I will choose hope over certainty. It's enough to begin.

Self-Betrayal Hurts Because You Care

The next few days are about rebuilding a relationship with yourself after you've disappointed yourself. How do you pick yourself up when your choices, actions, or inactions didn't match who you wanted to be? We often think trust is something others have to earn, but it's also something we must gently build with ourselves. These pages are about returning to self-loyalty without pretending you've never made mistakes.

That sinking feeling after you let yourself down? It's not proof that you're doomed. It's proof that you care. If you didn't care about your values, your goals, or your integrity, it wouldn't sting. The pain of self-betrayal means there's still something in you that wants to show up better. That's the seed of your healing.

Think of a time you disappointed yourself. What did that moment reveal about what you do value?

Just for this evening, I will see my regret as a sign of what matters rather than as a verdict of failure.

Day 232

Your Inner Critic Isn't Always Right
The voice in your head might sound confident when it tells you you're a screw-up. It might even use your past against you. That doesn't mean it's telling the truth. Your inner critic is often the internal echo of old experiences and not a reliable narrator. You're allowed to challenge that voice. You're allowed to say, "maybe you're wrong about me."

What's something your inner critic says that you've started to question?

Just for this evening, I will not confuse the loudest voice in my head with the truest one.

Self-Trust Is Rebuilt One Small Promise at a Time
You don't have to make a grand gesture to start trusting yourself again. You can begin with something tiny, like brushing your teeth, answering a text, or drinking a glass of water when you said you would. Each time you follow through on a small promise, your nervous system learns: I can count on myself again. That's how you rebuild the bridge.

What's one small promise you could make to yourself today and actually keep?

Just for this evening, I will let small wins count.

Day 234

You Can Forgive Yourself Without Letting Yourself Off the Hook
Forgiveness doesn't mean pretending it didn't happen. It doesn't mean ignoring harm. It means recognizing what went wrong and deciding not to live in permanent punishment mode. You can take responsibility, make repair, and still say, "I am more than this mistake." The balance of honesty without cruelty is what real self-forgiveness looks like.

Is there something you've been afraid to forgive yourself for because it felt like "letting yourself off easy?"

Just for this evening, I will believe that accountability and compassion can coexist.

You're Still Worthy of Leading Yourself

After a mistake, you might feel like you no longer deserve to guide your own life. You might feel like you're unqualified to make good decisions. Take note: you are still your best leader. You have insight now. You've seen what doesn't work. That doesn't make you less equipped. It makes you wiser. You can trust yourself again. You are allowed to trust yourself again.

What have your mistakes taught you that you wouldn't have learned otherwise?

Just for this evening, I will practice trusting the version of me that has grown.

Day 236

You Don't Have to Prove You've Changed to Be Changing
Sometimes we think we need visible evidence like a life overhaul, a clean slate, or a dramatic shift to prove we've changed. Most change starts invisibly. It starts in a decision. It starts in a quiet moment of choosing differently. The absence of proof doesn't mean you're not growing. Sometimes the most profound shifts are the ones no one can see yet ... not even you.

What's a quiet change you've made recently that others might not notice, but you're proud of?

Just for this evening, I will believe in the change I feel, even before it's obvious to others.

Regret ≠ Self-Hatred

Regret doesn't mean you deserve to punish yourself or disappear into shame. Feeling that ache usually means you've grown and can see more clearly than you could before. Your past is something to learn from, not something to use against yourself.

What's something you regret? What does it reveal about how much you've grown since?

Just for this evening, I will let regret remind me that I've changed and not condemn me for who I was

Day 238

Self-Hatred Isn't Accountability
Beating yourself up can feel like taking responsibility. It isn't. It's a trap that keeps you stuck in guilt without moving toward repair or renewal. Real accountability is constructive. It seeks to make things right. Self-hatred just breaks you down. You're allowed to take responsibility and still speak to yourself kindly.

Where in your life have you confused self-hatred with responsibility?

Just for this evening, I will not mistake cruelty for accountability.

You're More Than the Worst Thing You've Done

Everyone messes up. Everyone has a moment they wish they could undo. Your worth isn't erased by your worst day. You are more than a headline from your past. You are a whole story. Remember, the most beautiful chapters often come after the fall.

What's a story you're afraid others might reduce you to and how would you write the rest?

Just for this evening, I will not let one page define the book.

Day 240

You Don't Have to Hate Your Old Self to Love Who You Are Now
You can honor your growth without shaming your past. You can look at the younger version of yourself and say, "you were doing the best you could with what you knew." Sometimes the most healing thing is to thank your old self, including the messy parts, for getting you here.

What would you say to a younger version of yourself if you were feeling kind instead of critical?

Just for this evening, I will send love backward in time.

Regret Is Meant to Teach, Not Trap

When regret becomes a loop, it stops being useful. When you pause and ask what it's trying to teach you, it becomes a guide. Regret can sharpen your values, clarify your boundaries, and make your next decision braver. That's its gift. You don't have to stay stuck in the regret. You just listen to it, learn from it, and move on.

What has one of your regrets tried to teach you and have you learned it?

Just for this evening, I will let regret finish its lesson and leave the classroom.

Day 242

You Don't Have to Keep Picking Up the Knife to Stab Yourself
Some memories will always be tender, but they don't have to control how you see yourself. Caring for yourself means holding your story with honesty instead of punishment. Sometimes dwelling in past pain is you punishing yourself. You are allowed to put the knife of past pain down and look at it rather than pick it up and hurt yourself all over again. You are allowed to move forward gently, even with scars you don't fully understand yet.

What is something from the past that you may be re-wounding yourself with? What might it look like to gently accept that it happened and move forward without the pain?

Just for this evening, I will not let the guilt, shame or embarrassment of a past regret ruin my peace now.

You're Still Worthy, Even When You're Wounded

Regret doesn't have to be carried like a punishment, and you don't have to be fixed to be worthy. This chapter was about learning how to show yourself care, especially when you feel messy, hurt, or unsure. You are still someone worth showing up for, even in the middle of your imperfections.

What part of self-compassion has been hardest for you? What part has surprised you?

Just for this evening, I will carry my mistakes like compost. Yes, they are messy, but they are also rich with the potential to grow something beautiful.

Managing Emotional Overwhelm Without Numbing Out

Welcome to the Storm
You don't need to be fearless to face big emotions. You just need to stay. That's harder than it sounds, especially in a world full of ways to numb out. Numbing is a signal. It tells you you're past your emotional limit. This chapter is about learning to recognize those moments and stay present enough to get through them.

When you start to feel overwhelmed, what do you usually do? How does that make you feel afterward?

Just for this evening, I will acknowledge overwhelm is a signal that I need care.

Day 245

Your Future Self Isn't Disappointed in You

Emotional growth doesn't come from pretending you're fine. It comes from learning to sit with discomfort instead of immediately reaching for distraction. You don't need to be perfect. You just need to stay. Your future self isn't embarrassed by your struggles. Your future self exists because you kept going, even when things were messy.

What's one thing you've done recently that your future self might thank you for, even if it didn't look perfect?

Just for this evening, I will remember that I don't have to be who I used to be. I can keep becoming.

You Can't Manage What You Don't Notice

Overwhelm doesn't always shout. Sometimes it shows up quietly inside your body and thoughts. I t can look like tension, numbness, irritability, or exhaustion that slowly builds over time. The first step isn't fixing it. It's seeing it clearly without turning on yourself.

How does overwhelm show up in your body, thoughts, or behavior?

Just for this evening, I will practice noticing without judging.

Day 247

Your Nervous System Isn't Overreacting. It's Overloaded.
Your nervous system isn't trying to ruin your day. It's trying to protect you. When you feel flooded, frozen, angry, or shut down, it's because your system believes you've hit your limit. Nothing about that is weakness. It's your body trying to keep you safe.

What does nervous system overload feel like in your body?

Just for this evening, I will accept my nervous system is trying to protect me.

Everyone Has a Capacity and Yours Deserves Respect

You were never meant to push forever without rest or recovery. Emotional limits are real, and respecting them is a form of strength. It's certainly not failure. When you slow down instead of forcing yourself through, you are actually protecting your future self.

When have you pushed past your limit and paid for it later?

Just for this evening, I will remember respecting my limits helps me grow safely.

Day 249

Overwhelm Often Wears the Mask of "I'm Fine"

"I'm fine" can be a habit so familiar that you stop noticing when it isn't true. Hiding your feelings from yourself takes more energy than feeling them honestly ever could. Real relief starts when you let yourself admit what hurts quietly and safely.

What's something you've been pretending you're fine about?

Just for this evening, I will I let honesty soften the pressure I've been carrying.

You're Not Broken for Feeling This Much

Big feelings don't make you dramatic, behind, or failing at life. They mean you care, you're awake, and you're deeply human. You don't have to shrink your emotional world just to be easier to handle.

What's something you're carrying that feels heavier than it looks?

Just for this evening, I will not confuse sensitivity with weakness.

Day 251

Numbing Is a Survival Strategy

Numbing didn't come from nowhere. It grew out of moments when things felt too much to carry. It was your brain trying to protect you the only way it knew how at the time. Understanding this helps you replace shame with curiosity instead of punishment.

What numbing behaviors do you turn to most often?

Just for this evening, I will meet my coping habits with curiosity, not shame.

Distraction Isn't Always the Enemy

Not every distraction is unhealthy or wrong. Sometimes stepping away gives your system space to breathe and reset. The real question is whether you come back to yourself with kindness afterward.

When does distraction help you reset, and when does it disconnect you?

Just for this evening, I will notice whether I'm escaping or replenishing.

Day 253

Avoidance Steals Your Voice

Avoidance doesn't make pain disappear. It just makes you smaller around it. Over time, silence becomes a habit that slowly disconnects you from what matters. Your voice doesn't need to be loud, it just needs to be honest with yourself.

What truth have you been avoiding because it feels too big to handle?

Just for this evening, I will let my truth surface without rushing to fix it.

The False Comfort of Control
Control can feel safe when the inside of you feels chaotic. Planning, organizing, and perfecting often show up as armor instead of peace. The tighter you grip, the heavier everything starts to feel.

What do you try to control when you feel out of control inside?

Just for this evening, I will loosen my grip without losing myself.

Day 255

What You Reach for When You Can't Reach Yourself
Whether it's food, watching endless television, shopping, alcohol, or overworking, most numbing behaviors are a form of self-soothing. The things you reach for in overwhelm are not moral failures. They're signals. They show you what you're craving: safety, comfort, presence, or relief. When you see them with compassion, you begin to learn what you actually need. Learning to soothe with presence takes practice.

What do you reach for when you're overwhelmed, and what do you actually need in those moments?

Just for this evening, I will ask myself, "what am I needing right now?"

If Numbing Worked, You'd Be at Peace by Now
If your go-to coping method worked long-term, you wouldn't still feel this drained. Numbing is a pause. It's not the solution. You deserve more than temporary relief. You deserve true repair and recovery.

What would it look like to stop numbing just for today?

Just for this evening, I will be brave enough to stay with what is without reaching for temporary relief.

Day 257

Presence Can Be Built in Seconds
You don't need a 30-minute meditation to be present. Sometimes, just placing a hand on your chest and taking one real breath is enough to interrupt the spiral. Presence is a skill that grows from small reps.

What's one small way you could help yourself come back to the moment today?

Just for this evening, I will take one full, deep breath on purpose.

Safe Doesn't Always Mean Comfortable
Sometimes staying with your emotions feels less safe than avoiding them. Comfort and safety aren't always the same thing. You can be uncomfortable and safe enough to stay.

What emotions feel unsafe to you, and what would make them safer to sit with?

Just for this evening, I will notice what's uncomfortable without running.

Day 259

Emotional Intensity Isn't Permanent

No feeling lasts forever. Even the most overwhelming waves lose power when you stop feeding them panic. This is how you ride it through: name the emotion, ground your body in the present, and wait. The emotion will subside.

What emotion have you survived before that felt unbearable at the time?

Just for this evening, I will ride the wave, not drown in it.

Stay Until the Feeling Softens
Most people bail right before the feeling passes. That's when the panic peaks. That's when presence matters most. If you can stay for a minute longer, you might find relief without escape.

What's one feeling you usually numb or avoid? What might it be trying to tell you?

Just for this evening, I will remember I can pause instead of panic.

Day 261

Be With Yourself Like You'd Be With a Friend
You don't abandon your best friend when they're sobbing. You sit near them. You get them water. You say, "I'm here." Your body and heart deserve the same kindness.

How can you sit with yourself the way you'd sit with someone you love?

Just for this evening, I will stay beside myself and not against myself.

Staying With Yourself Builds Self-Trust
Every time you stay present instead of abandoning yourself, you build trust. You show your body that you can handle this. You show your brain that don't need to disappear. That's how you become your own safe place.

When was a time you showed up for yourself emotionally, even a little?

Just for this evening, I will accept I am becoming someone I can count on.

Day 263

Staying Doesn't Mean Solving

You don't have to fix every feeling. Just noticing it, naming it, and being kind to yourself is the work. Feelings want your attention, not your solutions.

What emotion is asking to be seen … and not solved … today?

Just for this evening, I will listen without fixing.

Make Space, Don't Shrink

When overwhelm hits, we often shrink ourselves. We use small words, quiet voice, and hide-away energy. You deserve more space when things feel big. So, stretch. Speak. Take up room.

What's one way you can make space for yourself today?

Just for this evening, I will not make myself smaller to survive.

Day 265

Move Your Body to Move the Feeling
Feelings live in your body. Gentle movement like stretching, walking, or even dancing can shake loose what words cannot. It's not about "working out." It's about moving through in a healthy manner.

What kind of movement helps you release tension, even a little?

Just for this evening, I will move something in my body to move something in my heart.

Expression Is the Opposite of Suppression
Crying, journaling, or singing loudly in your car provide exits for what's too big to hold inside. You weren't meant to bottle it all up. You're allowed to let it out.

What self-expression method helps you let go instead of shut down?

Just for this evening, I will give myself permission to feel out loud.

Day 267

You Don't Need a Full Plan to Take One Step
Emotional overwhelm can paralyze. You wait for the perfect plan before acting, but movement creates clarity. Taking one kind step forward is often all you need to begin again.

What is one tiny next step you can take without already having a full plan?

Just for this evening, I will trust myself to take one next step.

Grounding Anchors You When You Drift

Grounding techniques can interrupt the spiral. Try jumping into cold water or splashing some on your face. Try naming five things you see, smell, and hear. Try feeling your heartbeat in each of your ten fingertips and toes. Try completely relaxing your tongue. Any of these, along with so many other techniques, can interrupt the overwhelm spiral in your mind. These tiny rituals can bring you back to now.

What grounding tools work best for you when you start to drift?

Just for this evening, I will anchor myself gently back to this moment.

Day 269

Noticing Joy Amid Overwhelm Isn't Denial

Even when things feel too big, small joys still count. A smile from a stranger uplifts. The way your blanket feels comforts. Joy doesn't erase your pain. It reminds you there's still more to your story.

What small joy made itself known to you today?

Just for this evening, I will let myself notice one joyful thing.

Emotionally Present Doesn't Mean Emotionally Perfect

You don't have to do this flawlessly. Managing overwhelm isn't about control. It's about gentleness, noticing, and returning. You'll numb sometimes, but you'll also come back.

How have you come back to yourself lately, even after disconnecting?

Just for this evening, I will keep returning without shame.

Day 271

You Can Choose a Different Pattern Now

Sometimes, we repeat our overwhelm habits not because they work but because they're familiar. Here's the truth: your brain is always capable of learning something new. Every time you pause before falling into a default habit like doomscrolling, isolating, or over-apologizing, you interrupt the old pattern and open the door to a new one. That's how change begins: not with perfection, but with a pause.

What's a pattern you often fall into when overwhelmed? What's one small way you could respond differently next time?

Just for this evening, I will pause long enough to choose.

You're Allowed to Feel More Than One Thing at Once
You can be overwhelmed and still grateful. You can be numb and still trying. You can be hopeful and still hurting. Emotional complexity is normal humanness. Part of managing big emotions is giving yourself permission to feel contradictory things without trying to force one to cancel the other.

What are two seemingly opposite emotions you've felt today? What do they each want you to know?

Just for this evening, I will let all of my feelings have a voice, even if they don't all agree.

Day 273

Being With Your Emotions

This chapter wasn't about never numbing again. It was about building trust, softness, and presence, little by little. Emotional overwhelm is part of being human. And now, you've got tools, awareness, and new language to help tackle it. Most importantly, you've proven to yourself that you can stay.

What surprised you most about how you managed your emotions over the course of the last thirty days?

Just for this evening, I will say aloud, "I am not afraid of my feelings anymore. I can be with them and still be me."

Asking for Help
Without Feeling Like a Failure

Welcome to Asking for Help Like an Adult

You've probably heard "it's okay to ask for help" a hundred times from your parents, your teachers, your coaches and your bosses. That doesn't mean it feels okay to have to ask for help. This may be especially if you've grown up in environments where self-sufficiency was praised and vulnerability was misunderstood as weakness.

In this chapter, we'll gently unpack the stories you've been told about asking for help. We'll replace them with a deeper truth: interdependence is not only normal, it's necessary. You're not stupid or broken for needing others. You're a normal human being.

What messages did you receive growing up (directly or indirectly) about asking for help?

Just for this evening, I will acknowledge it's not weak to need support. It's wise to know when I do.

Day 275

When You Were the One Who Had to Be Okay

Some of us learned not to ask for help because we were never really allowed to need it. You might have been the oldest sibling, the "responsible one," or the emotional anchor for someone else's chaos. When that happens, needing anything can feel like failure or, worse, like being a burden. If this sounds like you, pay attention: you're allowed to need, too, even if you've always been the one others needed.

What roles did you have to play in your family or early life that made it hard to ask for help?

Just for this evening, I will remember needing help doesn't make me high-maintenance.

Asking for Help Doesn't Make You Less Capable

Being competent doesn't mean doing everything alone. In fact, one of the strongest things you can do is delegate. Think about the people you admire. They probably don't do everything themselves. So why should you have to? Needing help isn't the opposite of strength. It's part of how you stay strong.

What's one thing you're carrying right now that might feel lighter if you shared it?

Just for this evening, I will let myself imagine what ease might feel like.

Day 277

The Lie That Help Will Always Be Used Against You
Sometimes we don't ask for help because someone once made us regret it. Maybe they threw it in our face later, made us feel ashamed, or used it to control us. If that's happened to you, no wonder you're cautious. Here's the truth: not everyone will weaponize your vulnerability. Learning to ask again starts with learning to discern, not learning to never need.

What's a memory you carry about help being used to hurt you? What might you need to unlearn from that experience?

Just for this evening, I will honor my caution, but I won't confuse it with truth.

Not Everyone Is Watching You Struggle
Overwhelm can come with a strange kind of spotlight effect. It may seem like everyone can see how much you're drowning and is silently judging you for not handling it better. Most people are far more focused on their own lives than your to-do list. People usually aren't watching to criticize. If they are, they're not your people.

What pressure do you feel to appear like you're managing just fine?

Just for this evening, I will give myself permission to drop the act that I have it all together if I don't.

Day 279

You're Not the Exception to the Rule of Needing Help

You might believe that other people are allowed to ask for help, while you should have it together by now. This belief usually comes from perfectionism or trauma. It's not reality. There is no rulebook that says everyone gets to have needs except you. You're not the exception.

What stories do you tell yourself about being the one who's supposed to have it all together?

Just for this evening, I will treat my needs like they matter, because they do.

Interdependence: Independence Isn't the Only Way to Be Strong
You were never meant to do everything alone. Strength can look like connection, support, and shared weight instead of silent struggle. The next few days is dedicated to learning that needing others doesn't make you weak. It makes you part of the fabric of human life.

Who are three people you admire? How have they received help from others to get where they are?

Just for this evening, I will start to notice how strength and support often go hand in hand.

Day 281

Your Needs Aren't Inconvenient
When you've been made to feel like a bother, it can be hard to believe that anyone wants to help you. Love isn't a transaction. It's an invitation to be seen, heard, and supported. The people who love you want to show up for you. The hard part is letting them.

When have you stopped yourself from asking for help because you didn't want to "be a burden?"

Just for this evening, I will imagine what it would feel like to let someone show up for me without guilt.

Community Doesn't Make You Weak

The idea that we're supposed to be "self-made" is a fantasy. Even in your most isolated moments, your life is touched by other people's labor, kindness, and care. Giving and receiving in community is how humans survive.

What's one way you benefit from someone else's unseen support every day?

Just for this evening, I will honor the truth that we are built for connection, not isolation.

Day 283

It's Okay to Need Different Kinds of Support

Not every kind of help looks the same. Sometimes you need a venting buddy. Sometimes you need someone to send a funny meme. Sometimes you need help paying rent. All of these are valid. Don't downplay your needs just because they don't fit some "crisis" mold. You don't have to be drowning to deserve a life raft.

What kinds of support do you tend to minimize in your own life?

Just for this evening, I will give myself permission to need what I need, even if it feels small.

Being Vulnerable Is a Form of Courage

It's a lot easier to stay behind a wall than it is to open up and say, "I'm struggling." However, vulnerability creates magic. When you share your truth, you build intimacy, rather than pity. People connect through shared truths, not perfect facades. Vulnerability isn't weakness. It's risk wrapped in self-love, and every risk requires bravery.

What's one way you've bravely shared your truth, even if it felt scary?

Just for this evening, I will remind myself that courage often looks like asking.

Day 285

Everyone's Learning This Too

You're not the only one who struggles to ask for help. So many people around you are faking it, quietly overwhelmed, and scared to be seen as incapable. When you practice asking, you model something radical: it's okay to need. That alone makes space for others to be honest, too.

What would shift if you believed you weren't alone in this?

Just for this evening, I will remember that every time I ask for help, I make it easier for someone else to do the same.

Start Small, Stay Safe

You don't have to begin by revealing your deepest needs. Start with small, safe asks that build trust in yourself and others over time. Learning to ask for help is like building a muscle. You grow stronger through gentle, consistent practice.

What's one small thing you could ask for this week that wouldn't feel too scary?

Just for this evening, I will practice one tiny ask, even just for a favor that isn't urgent.

Day 287

Create an "Ask Script"

Sometimes, not knowing how to ask keeps us silent. Having a go-to phrase can lower the emotional barrier. Try: "I'm not sure how to say this, but I could use a little support with..." or "can I talk through something with you?" Scripts aren't inauthentic. They're a form of scaffolding when your heart is wobbly.

Write out a sentence or two you could use to ask for help the next time you need it.

Just for this evening, I will try saying my script out loud to myself. I will let it feel real in my mouth.

It's Not Your Job to Manage Their Reaction

When you ask for help, you might start mentally running through how the other person might respond. What if they feel burdened? What if they say no? What if they think less of you? Your job is to honor your own needs. It's not to pre-edit your vulnerability for someone else's comfort. Their reaction is theirs. Your courage is yours.

What do you fear people will think of you if you ask for help?

Just for this evening, I will remind myself that I can't control others' reactions.

Day 289

Rejection Doesn't Mean You Shouldn't Have Asked
Sometimes you do ask, and the answer is "no." That hurts. It doesn't mean you were wrong to ask. It doesn't mean you were too much. It just means they couldn't give what you needed at that moment. That's disappointing, not shameful. The ask itself was brave.

Has a rejection ever made you stop asking altogether? What did it teach you and what did it not have to teach you?

Just for this evening, I will honor the courage it took me to ask, regardless of the outcome.

Choose the Right Person, Not the Closest One
Not everyone is safe to ask … and that's okay. Just because someone is nearby doesn't mean they're your best bet. Pay attention to who listens well, who doesn't interrupt, and who follows through. Asking for help wisely isn't about being desperate. It's about being discerning.

Who in your life has shown you they are emotionally safe to ask for support?

Just for this evening, I will remember that I can't go to the bread store for ice cream.

Day 291

Helping Builds Connection, Not Debt
You might hesitate to ask because you don't want to "owe" someone. Healthy relationships aren't ledgers. Helping is a form of connection, not a transaction. If someone offers you help joyfully, your "repayment" is simply letting yourself be loved.

When has someone helped you freely, without making you feel like you were in debt?

Just for this evening, I will let go of the idea that receiving help means I now owe something in return.

It's Okay to Feel Weird About Being Helped

Receiving help can feel awkward, vulnerable, and unfamiliar, even when it's freely given. You might feel guilt, hesitation, or an urge to pull back, and that doesn't mean you're doing it wrong. Feeling strange about being supported is often a sign that you're learning something new and brave.

What comes up for you emotionally when someone offers help without hesitation?

Just for this evening, I will allow the discomfort of being cared for and stay with it instead of running.

Day 293

Stop Shrinking Your Gratitude to Hide Your Shame
Sometimes we say "thank you" with a grimace instead of genuine warmth. Why? Because when we feel ashamed, even gratitude can get twisted. You don't have to overcompensate or act like someone saved your life to be thankful. Say thank you like someone who knows they're worth helping, not someone trying to earn it retroactively.

Think of a time you said thank you but didn't really feel it. What was getting in the way?

Just for this evening, I will practice saying "thank you" without shrinking, just once.

You're Allowed to Receive Without Explaining Everything
There's a reflex that kicks in when someone helps us. We start over-explaining why we needed it. We justify, over-disclose, or backpedal. Explanation isn't a prerequisite for compassion. If someone offers help, you don't have to build a PowerPoint of your pain to accept it. Let your "yes, thank you" be enough.

What do you tend to over-explain when you're feeling vulnerable?

Just for this evening, I will remind myself that I don't owe anyone a full backstory just to be worthy of kindness.

Day 295

You Don't Have to Return the Favor Right Away

One of the fastest ways to block real connection is to turn a gift into a transaction. If someone helps you and your first instinct is to immediately repay them, pause. Healthy relationships have rhythms of giving and receiving that don't need to be one-for-one. Let it be okay to simply accept.

When have you tried to "balance the books" emotionally? How did that feel?

Just for this evening, I will let kindness land, without trying to match it or outdo it right away.

Notice How Others Receive Support Without Guilt

Sometimes, it's easier to spot grace in others than ourselves. Watch how people you care about ask for help or how they receive help. Imagine if you treated yourself the same way. Let their ease remind you what's possible. Let their stumbles remind you that it's okay to learn.

Think of someone who receives help well. What can you learn from them?

Just for this evening, I will allow myself to be a student of receiving.

Day 297

There's No Such Thing as "Too Much" Help

You might fear that you'll cross a line and that one more ask will tip you into "too needy." Real support systems aren't keeping tallies. If you're still struggling, it means you're still in need. It doesn't mean that you've maxed out your worthiness. You are not a quota.

When do you start worrying that you're "too much?" Where did that message come from?

Just for this evening, I will remind myself that asking again does not make me a failure.

Redefining Strength

Strength isn't about doing everything alone. Real independence includes knowing when to stand on your own and when to lean on others. Asking for help doesn't weaken you. It strengthens your foundation.

How have you confused "doing it alone" with being strong?

Just for this evening, I will remind myself that needing support doesn't cancel out my independence.

Day 299

Your Vulnerability is a Gift

When you ask for help, you give others a chance to love you. You show that you trust them. That's not a burden. It's a gift. Vulnerability invites closeness. People want to be needed by those they care about. Don't rob them of that chance by keeping it all inside.

When has someone made you feel honored by trusting you with their need?

Just for this evening, I will let myself believe that I am worthy of support and love just as I am.

Help Doesn't Have to Be Perfect to Be Helpful

Sometimes people don't help you in the exact way you hoped. That doesn't mean they didn't try, and it doesn't mean it didn't count. Receiving imperfect help still counts as connection. It doesn't always solve the whole problem, but it reminds you that you're not alone.

Can you think of a time when help didn't "fix" things but still meant something?

Just for this evening, I will be open to support, even if it looks a little different than I imagined.

Day 301

Asking is a Leadership Skill

Think about the people you admire, like your mentors, teachers, and role models. Chances are, they didn't get there by white-knuckling everything alone. They built teams. They asked for mentorship. They raised their hands. Asking for help is actually a key trait of strong, smart leaders. The next time you reach out, remember that you're practicing leadership.

Who is someone you admire who's great at building support systems?

Just for this evening, I will remind myself that leaders don't do everything. They ask for what they need.

Build Your Personal Help Map

Everyone's support system looks different. Some people have tight-knit families. Others rely on friends, mentors, or even online communities. What matters is knowing who you can turn to and for what. Create a mental (or actual) map of your people. Who's safe for emotional venting? Who's great at practical help? Who just makes you laugh when you need it?

List three people you can ask for help. What kind of help do they tend to offer best.

Just for this evening, I will remind myself that I'm not alone . I have options, even if I sometimes forget.

Day 303

Your Future Self Will Thank You for Asking
When you're stuck, overwhelmed, or scared, asking for help can feel like a defeat. Every time you reach out, you're investing in your own well-being. You're building resilience. You're making it easier for the next version of you to keep growing. Future-you will be so grateful you didn't wait to be perfect or calm or certain and that you just asked.

What's one thing you might look back on later and be glad you asked for help with?

Just for this evening, I will take one tiny action today that future-me will be proud of.

What Did You Learn About Asking for Help?

You've just spent nearly thirty days unlearning some of the hardest messages to let go of … that needing help is weakness, that being supported means being a burden, and that independence means doing everything alone. But, look at you now! You've explored what help really means, how to receive it, and how to ask without shame. This work isn't about becoming dependent. It's about becoming whole. The next time life gets heavy (and it will), remember you don't have to carry it all alone.

What beliefs about help and asking have shifted for you as you completed this chapter? What's one habit you want to keep practicing?

Just for this evening, I will be proud of the ways I've grown, and I will carry forward what I've learned, one ask at a time.

Tolerating Boredom and Discomfort

Tolerating Boredom and Discomfort

Most of us have been trained to fear boredom, to fear silence and to fear discomfort of any kind. We're told to stay busy, stay distracted, and always feel "fine." Real life doesn't work that way. Discomfort is inevitable, and boredom is not the enemy. It's the birthplace of creativity, rest, and self-awareness. In this chapter, we're learning how to stay with yourself, with hard feelings, and with silence. You'll build tolerance, not just for discomfort, but for the quiet power that lives inside it.

What do you usually do when you feel bored or uncomfortable? Do you reach for your phone? Try to fix it? Numb out?

Just for this evening, I will remind myself that not every uncomfortable moment needs to be solved. Some just need to be witnessed.

Day 306

The Escape Button is Always There. You Don't Have to Press It. We live in a world full of escape hatches. One tap and you're somewhere else scrolling, swiping, shopping, and zoning out. It's not your fault that you developed habits around escaping boredom or pain. Here's the truth: you don't have to use the escape button every time. You can stay in the boredom. You can feel the boredom. You can wait it out, and you won't break.

What's your favorite "escape button?" How does it make you feel afterward?

Just for this evening, I will try sitting still for five minutes without reaching for my usual distraction.

Your Nervous System Isn't Broken

When discomfort hits, your body might panic, complete with racing thoughts, fidgeting, or a flood of shame. That doesn't mean you're weak or broken. It means your nervous system is doing its job in scanning for danger. Here's the thing: not all discomfort is danger. Some discomfort is just everyday human life. You can learn to remind your body that you're safe.

What sensations or thoughts usually come up when you feel uncomfortable?

Just for this evening, I will take three deep breaths and thank my body for trying to protect me.

Day 308

Avoiding Pain Can Create More of It

Avoidance feels good in the short-term, but it often stretches out the pain. That hard thing you didn't want to think about? It waits for you. The discomfort you numbed? It grows legs. Facing things directly can be tough, but it's usually faster and gentler than avoidance in the long run.

What's something you avoided recently that ended up getting worse?

Just for this evening, I will remind myself that I'm strong enough to face things I'd usually avoid.

The Lie of "I Should Always Feel Good"

You are not supposed to feel happy or productive all the time. Life is a mix of light and shadow, energy and fatigue, and clarity and confusion. When we expect to feel good all the time, we end up pathologizing natural dips. It's okay to have a flat day.

When you're not feeling "good," how do you usually treat yourself?

Just for this evening, I will let myself be exactly as I am with no fixing and no judging.

Day 310

You Don't Have to Earn Stillness

Somewhere along the way, we learn that rest, quiet, or slowness has to be earned. Do you feel like you can only chill if you've done something "worthy" that day? Boredom and stillness aren't luxuries or rewards. They're parts of being alive. You're allowed to stop and do nothing sometimes, just because.

What beliefs do you hold about being still, unproductive, or lazy?

Just for this evening, I will give myself permission to stop trying to earn the right to slow down.

The Tiny Window Where You Can Choose Again

There's a moment … a tiny window … between feeling uncomfortable and acting on that discomfort. Most of the time we miss it and go straight to distraction. If you can spot it, you can stretch it. You can pause. You can choose again. Freedom of choice lives in the space between impulse and intention.

Think of a time you paused before reacting? How did that feel?

Just for this evening, I will try to notice the next time I want to check out and pause instead.

Day 312

Boredom Isn't Emptiness. It's Space.
Boredom often gets mistaken for a void, like something is missing. Sometimes, it's actually space. Sometimes it's space your brain doesn't know how to fill yet. If you can tolerate that pause without racing to fix it, you might discover the beginnings of insight, creativity, or even calm. Boredom can be the prelude to something surprising, if you let it unfold.

When was the last time you let yourself be bored (like really, truly bored) without filling the space?

Just for this evening, I will let myself experience boredom as space and not as a failure to be entertained.

Day 313

The Gift of Wandering Attention

We treat wandering attention like a flaw, but it's actually how the brain resets. Studies show that when your mind drifts, it begins solving problems, stitching together ideas, and filing memories. Constant focus isn't always better. Boredom can be the starting line for imagination. Allow your mind to wander without shame.

What kinds of thoughts or ideas show up when you're zoning out?

Just for this evening, I will spend a few minutes letting my mind wander without steering it or judging it.

Day 314

Boredom as a Check Engine Light

Sometimes boredom is a clue. It's not that something is wrong with you, but that something needs attention. Maybe a value is being ignored. Maybe you're stuck in autopilot. Maybe you need a refresh. Boredom can be a nudge to re-engage with what matters.

What might your current boredom be trying to tell you?

Just for this evening, I will treat my boredom with curiosity instead of criticism.

The Difference Between Stimulus and Satisfaction

Our world is overflowing with stimulus, and not all of it is satisfying. Scrolling, clicking, and consuming can feel like activity, but it might not leave you feeling full. Real satisfaction often comes from doing less, not more. Let your boredom guide you toward something meaningful instead of just more noise.

What's something that leaves you overstimulated but undernourished?

Just for this evening, I will choose one simple, quiet thing that truly satisfies me instead of just another distraction.

Day 316

You Don't Have to Monetize or Master Your Boredom

Not every interest has to become a side hustle or a skill. You're allowed to be curious, to dabble, to try things just for fun. If you let yourself be bored, you might stumble into something playful. And, that something that doesn't need to be productive to be worthwhile.

What's something you're curious about that you've never given yourself permission to explore?

Just for this evening, I will do one small thing just because I want to … no outcome required.

The "Aha" Insights that Only Show Up in Silence

Some insights can't be summoned. They arrive quietly in the middle of the stillness you might be trying to avoid. If you can stay present during boredom, even just for a little while, your mind may hand you something unexpected. You might "receive" an idea, a feeling, or a truth. You don't have to force it. You just have to make space for it.

Have you ever had an important realization during a "boring" moment?

Just for this evening, I will spend a few minutes in stillness and see what rises up.

Day 318

The Stretch Zone vs. the Panic Zone
Growth happens just outside your comfort zone … but not way outside. There's a difference between being stretched and being overwhelmed. The stretch zone is where you're challenged but still feel safe enough to learn. The panic zone is where things feel too big, too fast, or too unsafe. Learning to tell the difference is key to building resilience without burnout.

Can you recall a time when you grew from discomfort and a time when it was just too much?

Just for this evening, I will check in with myself and ask, "am I being stretched right now… or pushed past my limits?"

Growing Pains Are Still Pains

"Growth mindset" is powerful. It doesn't mean growth is easy. Even when you're doing something good for yourself, it can feel awkward, exhausting, or emotional. That doesn't mean you're doing it wrong. Growing pains are real. They just mean you're changing.

Is there something you're working on that feels harder than you expected? What would it mean to call that "growth" instead of "struggle"?

Just for this evening, I will give myself credit for showing up, even when it's not graceful.

Day 320

Discomfort Can Be a Signal to Pause

It's easy to confuse discomfort with danger. Sometimes quitting feels like the only safe choice. Not all discomfort means "stop." Sometimes it means "slow down." Sometimes it means "breathe through it." Knowing when to pause instead of quit is one of the hardest and most adult skills you can develop.

What's something you gave up on because it felt too hard? How might you approach it differently now?

Just for this evening, I will ask myself gently, "do I need to stop, or do I need a breather?"

Day 321

Confidence Comes from Doing Hard Things Badly (At First)

Confidence isn't something you magically have. It's something you build. Confidence is made from raw materials: awkwardness, mess-ups, and tries that don't work. Doing hard things badly at first is how you learn to do them well. Every beginner is uncomfortable. That's not a failure. That's the price of admission.

What's something you're avoiding because you don't want to be bad at it?

Just for this evening, I will give myself permission to be a beginner … messy, clumsy, and brave.

Day 322

The Fear of Looking Silly

One of the sneakiest discomforts is embarrassment. We're terrified of looking silly, of doing the wrong thing, and of being seen failing. Living (and learning) happen as much in front of other people as in private. It's brave to show up and try anyway. Braver still to laugh at yourself and keep going.

When was the last time you stopped yourself from doing something because you were afraid of how it might look?

Just for this evening, I will remind myself that looking silly isn't the worst thing while missing out because of fear might be.

Day 323

Discomfort is Temporary While Growth is Lasting

In the moment, discomfort feels huge and never-ending. Here's some great news about discomfort: it passes. On the other side of it, there's strength, perspective, and confidence. Every time you stretch and come back safely, your nervous system learns that discomfort is survivable. That's how long-term resilience is built. It's not by avoiding pain but by moving through it.

What's a challenge you've lived through that shaped who you are?

Just for this evening, I will remind myself that the version of me I'm becoming is worth a little discomfort.

Day 324

The Urge to Escape

When discomfort creeps in, your brain immediately wants out. It quickly entices you to scroll, snack, sleep, ghost, and doom spiral. You don't need to beat yourself up for these instincts. They're just your human mind trying to protect you from uncomfortable feelings. Building emotional stamina means sometimes letting the feeling stay instead of fleeing it. The urge to escape is just that ... an urge. You don't have to obey it.

What's your go-to escape hatch when you feel emotionally overwhelmed?

Just for this evening, I will notice my urges without acting on them.

Naming is Calming

It's a strange but powerful truth: when you name a feeling, it loses some of its bite. Try saying your feeling out loud: "I'm anxious," "I'm disappointed" or "I'm lonely." Naming doesn't solve the emotion, but it shrinks the fog. It gives you a shape to work with. Staying gets easier when you can say out loud, "this is what's here."

What feeling are you most reluctant to name when it shows up?

Just for this evening, I will try naming what I'm feeling, gently and without judgment.

Day 326

You're Not Stuck, You're Pausing

Discomfort can trick you into believing you're stuck, that nothing's changing, and that you'll feel this way forever. Pause is not paralysis. Stillness isn't stagnation. Even when it feels like you're going nowhere, you're still metabolizing and healing.

When was a time you thought you were stuck but realized later you were just catching your breath?

Just for this evening, I will trust that even in stillness, something inside me is shifting.

Staying Isn't Suffering for Suffering's Sake
Staying present with discomfort doesn't mean you must sit in pain forever. The point isn't to prove anything or punish yourself. It's to learn how to hold feelings without needing to destroy them or yourself. You stay just long enough to learn what's underneath. Then you let go when you're ready.

How do you know when it's time to stay with something versus time to let go?

Just for this evening, I will give myself permission to feel and also to rest.

Day 328

You Can Feel Big Feelings and Still Be Okay

This might be the deepest truth of all: you can feel completely overwhelmed and still be okay. You can cry and still be strong. You can wobble and still be grounded. You are allowed to fall apart and also be whole. Big feelings are just that. They're big. They're not bad. They're not dangerous. They're just thoughts and they're just big.

What "big" feeling have you learned to tolerate more than you could a year ago?

Just for this evening, I will remember that I can feel hard things without breaking.

You Stayed

There have been so many moments while working through this chapter where you could've numbed out, tuned out and checked out. Instead, you stayed. Maybe not perfectly, but you practiced being with your own mind, your own emotions, and your own body. That's a huge deal. Staying isn't easy. And, now you know you can do it.

What have you discovered about by staying with your discomfort?

Just for this evening, I will honor the progress I've made.

Day 330

Boredom as a Signal Instead of a Failure

So many of us were raised to believe that boredom means we're lazy, ungrateful, or wasting time. Boredom is often a signal. Boredom is not a character flaw. It means your brain is seeking novelty, meaning, or alignment. When you learn to listen to boredom instead of fighting it, you open a door to creativity, self-reflection, and even change.

What do you think your boredom might be trying to tell you lately?

Just for this evening, I will pause and ask, "what unmet need might be hiding beneath this boredom?"

The Gift of Unstructured Time

In the rush of productivity culture, we often lose the art of doing nothing. Unstructured time is where ideas incubate, identities clarify, and your nervous system can reset. Discomfort in stillness is normal, and so is the peace that eventually follows, if you let yourself stay.

When was the last time you had truly unstructured time and how did it feel?

Just for this evening, I will give myself the gift of a few minutes with no plan, no goal, and no guilt.

Day 332

Redefining What Counts as "Progress"
Progress isn't always visible. Sometimes it looks like rest. Sometimes it looks like noticing instead of numbing. Sometimes it looks like choosing not to bolt. If you've stayed with hard moments this while working through this chapter, even briefly that's progress. If you've named an emotion you used to hide from, that's progress.

What invisible progress have you made that deserves to be acknowledged?

Just for this evening, I will honor the quiet victories I've earned.

You're the Kind of Person Who Can Stay

You've shown yourself something powerful: you can stay with awkward moments, restlessness, and tough emotions. You've learned that discomfort isn't your enemy. It might be your edge. You've discovered that you are not fragile. You are flexible. That's a kind of strength you'll carry forever.

What would change if you fully believed you are strong enough to stay?

Just for this evening, I will whisper to myself, "I'm still here. And I'm proud of that."

Day 334

What Did You Learn About Boredom and Discomfort?
You began this chapter with a challenge most people try to avoid: to feel the hard stuff without numbing out. Along the way, you discovered that boredom can be space. That discomfort can be a teacher. Staying present doesn't mean you're failing to cope. It means you're learning to live. You've built muscles that will carry you through future fog, frustration, and fidgety days. That's real adulting.

What strategy or shift are you most proud of learning from this chapter?

Just for this evening, I will carry this lesson forward: I can be here, with myself, even when it's hard.

Celebrating Small Wins and Noticing Progress

What If You're Already Doing Better Than You Think?
Sometimes success is loud and shouts with a diploma, a job, a breakup, or a move. More often, success whispers. It shows up when you choose kindness instead of defensiveness. It shows up when you take a breath instead of sending the angry text. It shows up when you try again after failing. This chapter isn't about proving yourself. It's about noticing how far you've already come, especially in the moments no one clapped for. If you've ever asked, "am I even making progress?" this chapter will help you see the answer with clearer eyes.

What's one quiet way you've grown this year, perhaps something subtle that others might not have noticed, but you know took work?

Just for this evening, I will treat my small wins like they matter, because they do.

Day 336

Redefining What Progress Looks Like

The world often praises big, flashy achievements, like the kind that earn applause or certificates. Real progress is often invisible. It's sending the email you've been avoiding. It's choosing to get out of bed when everything feels heavy. It's going to therapy, taking a walk, making a hard decision. Wins don't have to be wild to be worthy. They just have to be yours.

What's something you did recently that wouldn't look impressive to someone else but mattered deeply to you?

Just for this evening, I will honor my quiet wins, even if no one else sees them.

Wins Without Witnesses Still Count

If a tree falls in the forest and no one hears it, it still fell. If you made a brave choice and no one clapped, it's still brave. You don't need witnesses or validation to make something real. Part of growing up is learning to clap for yourself and learning that noticing your own efforts is enough.

What's something you did alone that you're proud of?

Just for this evening, I will see for myself what I did, and what I did is enough.

Day 338

Surviving Is Sometimes the Win
Some days, just getting through is an act of strength. There are days when showering, replying to one message, or just breathing through a panic spiral is the win. Not every season is about thriving. Sometimes, it's about surviving.

What kind of win have you survived lately, even if it looked like "nothing" on the outside?

Just for this evening, I will remind myself that getting through the day is a valid success.

Wins Can Be Rest, Too
Doing less is rarely praised. Learning to rest (really, truly rest) is a win, too. Especially if you come from a background where productivity was tied to worth. Choosing rest without shame is choosing self-trust. You're not lazy. You're learning to listen to yourself.

When was the last time you chose rest instead of pushing through? How did that feel?

Just for this evening, I will remember rest is not failure. It is repair.

Day 340

Effort That Doesn't "Work" Is Still Progress

Not everything you try will succeed. Trying counts. Sending the text even if it's left on read ... counts. Applying for the job even if you don't get it ... counts. Taking the first step even if you trip ... counts. Every time you act in alignment with your values, even if the outcome isn't ideal, you've moved forward.

What's something you attempted recently that didn't go perfectly but still moved you forward?

Just for this evening, I will give myself credit for trying, not just for "winning."

Self-Kindness Is a Win

You might think wins only happen when you're doing something. The way you talk to yourself counts, too. Every time you choose to speak kindly to yourself instead of spiraling into shame is a win. It builds inner trust. Over time, it becomes a habit that can change your whole life.

When did you last talk to yourself gently instead of harshly?

Just for this evening, I will remember the way I speak to myself is part of my progress.

Day 342

Progress Isn't Linear (And That's Okay)

You're not a machine. You're a person. People grow in spirals and not straight lines. Some days you'll feel like you're soaring. On other days, it's like you're back where you started. Great news: that zig-zag is still forward movement. Progress is allowed to have setbacks, pauses, and even detours.

What's one area of your life where progress hasn't been linear but has been real progress?

Just for this evening, I will keep moving onwards. A backward step doesn't erase all the steps I've taken forward.

Done is Better Than Perfect

Perfectionism often sounds like high standards, but really, it's fear in disguise. It's fear of being judged, failing, or not being enough. Finishing something at 70% is often more powerful than waiting until you can do it at 100%. You get better by doing and not by waiting to be perfect.

What's something you delayed or avoided because you were afraid it wouldn't be perfect?

Just for this evening, I will choose progress over perfection.

Day 344

Repeat Doesn't Mean "Fail"

If you find yourself needing to relearn the same lesson, welcome to adulthood. Growth often requires repetition. You'll forget and remember. You'll build and rebuild. That's not failure or stupidity. That's being a normal human adult. If you're showing up to re-learn again, that is progress.

What's something you've had to circle back to more than once? How has your approach changed?

Just for this evening, I will give myself permission to repeat without judgment.

Small Steps Count

When you imagine progress, your brain might default to big leaps. However, progress is often a slow accumulation of tiny choices. Progress is texting the friend back, showing up to class, or leaving the toxic group chat. It's what you do often (not what you do once) that creates change.

What's one small, repeated action that's helped you make progress this year?

Just for this evening, I will go slowly. Tiny steps still move me forward.

Day 346

Perfection Can Be a Distraction

Sometimes the goal of "doing it perfectly" keeps you from doing it at all. It becomes a stall tactic. If you wait to feel completely ready, confident, and competent, you might never take the leap. Remember that you don't have to be perfect to begin. So, just get yourself started already!

What have you been putting off because you think you're not ready enough yet?

Just for this evening, I will stop trying to be flawless in order to begin.

Being Present Is Progress, Too

When you're obsessed with the end goal, you can miss the joy of the journey that's happening right now. Sometimes just being present and truly noticing what you feel, what you need, and what's right in front of you at this moment is the work. You don't have to constantly push forward.

What's one way you stayed present with yourself today?

Just for this evening, I will embrace that growth happens in this moment and not just at the finish line.

Day 348

Start Noticing What's Working

Your brain is wired to scan for what's going wrong. It's an old survival trick, and it can make your life feel like an endless list of problems. What's the antidote? Practice noticing what's working, too. It's not delusion. It's brain balance. Recognizing what's going well builds hope, and it reminds you you're not stuck.

What's one thing, no matter how small, that's been going right lately?

Just for this evening, I will let myself feel what's working, not just what's broken.

Write Yourself a Note of Recognition

You probably know how to write an apology note or a thank-you note. What about a recognition note? Try one that says, "hey, I saw what you did, and that was awesome." You don't have to wait for someone else to say it. You can give that gift to yourself.

If you were writing a note to yourself, what would you want to be acknowledged for?

Just for this evening, I will seek outside permission to be proud of myself.

Day 350

Let Yourself Receive a Compliment

Have you ever brushed off a compliment with a joke or deflection? You're not alone, because most of us have. However, receiving kind words without shrinking or squirming is a skill. It allows you to absorb love, not just survive on self-critique. Practice letting praise land.

What's a compliment you've heard recently that you'd like to believe more fully?

Just for this evening, I will let in the goodness someone sees in me.

Day 351

Make a Ritual Out of Noticing Progress
You don't need a big event to recognize growth. A ritual could be lighting a candle once a week and naming one thing you're proud of. It could be a playlist, a journal entry, or a walk. Rituals give shape to what matters. They say: this moment is worth remembering.

What small weekly or monthly ritual could help you honor your own growth?

Just for this evening, I will slow down. Progress deserves pause and ritual.

Day 352

Celebrate With a Gift to Future You
Sometimes, the best way to recognize growth is to leave something behind for your future self. This could be a note, a reminder, a playlist or even a dollar in a coat pocket. It doesn't have to be big. It can just be something that says, "I see you. And I believe in where you're headed."

What gift could you leave for your future self to remind them how far you've come?

Just for this evening, I will pay it forward. My future me deserves love from today's me.

Reflect on a Time You Thought You'd Never Get Through

Look back … really look. Was there a time this year when you thought, I can't do this, and then you did? Those moments are often buried by the urgency of the next thing. Today, pause and name it. You got through something hard. That's worth honoring.

What's a hard time you survived and what inner resources helped you make it through?

Just for this evening, I will celebrate that getting through it was a kind of brilliance, too.

Day 354

You're Becoming Easier to Be With (Even to Yourself)

Sometimes the most important progress is internal. It's not in what you accomplish, but in how you treat yourself along the way. Maybe you catch yourself with more patience now. Maybe you don't spiral as far when things go wrong. This quiet kindness builds a more peaceful relationship with yourself, and that makes everything else feel a little lighter.

In what ways have you become a calmer, kinder presence in your own life?

Just for this evening, I will embrace learning how to live alongside myself with more ease.

The Way You Walk Through Life Is Different Now

It's not just about what you've done. It's about how you move. Maybe you breathe before reacting now. Maybe you check in with yourself instead of people-pleasing. Maybe you rest before burning out. These are meaningful shifts in how you walk through the world.

What's one small behavioral change that reflects your internal growth?

Just for this evening, I will keep in mind the way I move through the world is part of who I'm becoming.

Day 356

You Don't Owe Anyone the Old Version of You

Sometimes the people around you still expect the "old you." They are expecting the one who stayed quiet, said yes to everything, and didn't speak up. It can feel hard to grow when others resist your change. You don't owe anyone a performance of your past self. You get to be renewed.

What's one old version of yourself you've outgrown? Are ready to let go of?

Just for this evening, I will release the need to keep playing a role I've outgrown.

Self-Trust Grows with Repetition

Trusting yourself doesn't come from saying the right things. It comes from showing up for yourself repeatedly. Every time you follow through on a boundary, speak kindly to yourself, or take a healthy risk, you're strengthening your self-trust muscle. Keep practicing.

What's something you've done more consistently this year that's helped you build trust with yourself?

Just for this evening, I will embrace becoming someone I can rely on.

Day 358

You Can Define Your Own Success

Maybe success isn't a job title or a relationship status. Maybe it's being able to sleep at night. Maybe it's laughing freely. Maybe ti's having the courage to start over. You get to decide what matters and build a life that reflects your definition of thriving.

What does success look like for you now? How has that changed?

Just for this evening, I will be firm that my definition of success gets to fit me, not anyone else.

You're Still Becoming (and That's a Good Thing)

You don't have to "arrive" to be worthy of celebration. You're still in motion and still evolving. That means there's more room to grow, learn, shift, and stretch. Becoming isn't a race to the finish. It's the long, winding journey of a lifetime lived.

What kind of person are you becoming, not just in terms of what you do, but how you show up?

Just for this evening, I will be proud of who I'm becoming, even if I'm not there yet.

Day 360

You Can Start Again Any Time

There will be days when you forget everything you've learned. There will be days when you spiral. There will be days when you ghost your growth. That doesn't mean you didn't succeed. Starting again doesn't require a Monday, or a new month, or a journal prompt. It only takes a breath and a choice.

When you lose your way, what helps you begin again?

Just for this evening, I will accept a reset is always possible. I am always allowed to begin again.

Take Stock of the Tools You Want to Keep

This journal offered you dozens of tools: grounding techniques, self-reflections, mindset shifts, and rituals of recognition, amongst others. Not all of them were for you, and that's okay. Some of them probably landed. This is the moment to take stock. Choose what fits. Leave what doesn't. Carry what serves you.

Which tools, prompts, or habits from this year actually helped? How could you keep using them?

Just for this evening, I will gather what works and let the rest go.

Day 362

Build Your Own Support Net

You don't have to be self-sufficient to be strong. You just need to know how to reach. Friends, therapists, playlists, places, rituals, and mantras are all part of your support net. When you feel yourself slipping, you can lean on it instead of falling through.

Who or what is part of your support net right now? Where might you want to add to it?

Just for this evening, I will reach out. I'm not meant to carry everything alone.

Make It Easy to Remember What You've Learned

Growth sticks best when it's easy to access. That could mean saving favorite prompts, writing a mantra on your mirror, or screenshotting a few reflections that hit hard. Learning to care for yourself is powerful. And, learning how to remember it on tough days is the real trick.

What's one way you can make your favorite lesson or tool from this year easy to access when you need it?

Just for this evening, I will help myself make my learnings easier to find.

Day 364

You're the One Who Did This
The journal helped. The prompts helped. Yet, you're the one who came back to the page, again and again. You asked hard questions. You sat in your feelings. You grew. This is your work, your win, your unfolding. No one gets to take that from you.

What part of yourself are you most proud of for sticking with this?

Just for this evening, I will give myself kudos. I did this. I am the one who chose to grow.

Look at You Now

A year ago, you opened this journal not knowing where it would take you. Maybe you were excited. Maybe you were overwhelmed. Maybe you were just curious. And, here you are … 365 days later. You're growing. You're choosing yourself. You're showing up with tenderness and grit, even on the hard days. You've learned to sit with discomfort. You've gotten honest with yourself. You've practiced celebrating the tiniest wins and being gentler when you screw up. That is no small thing.

If you've forgotten entries, skipped days, or cried your way through pages, that's okay. If it took you two years instead of one to get here, that's okay, too. That's life. This wasn't a test. It was a companion. Now you get to carry all of it forward. You get to carry it forward not as a set of rules, but as proof that you are capable of reflection, compassion, and progress.

You didn't finish this journal perfectly. You finished it honestly. And guess what? If you wanted to, you could start this journal all over again.

Imagine the you who will open this journal again in a year, or five. What do you want them to remember about the you who's finishing it today? What do you hope they're still holding onto, still believing and still growing into?

Just for this evening, I will be so proud of myself. I finished something that mattered. I'm not done growing … not even close. I know how to keep going now. I am someone who shows up in my own life.

www.ingramcontent.com/pod-product-compliance
Lightning Source LLC
Chambersburg PA
CBHW051244250726
48656CB00004B/1113